INCLUSIFY

INCLUSIFY

The Power of Uniqueness and Belonging to Build Innovative Teams

STEFANIE K. JOHNSON

HARPER
BUSINESS

An Imprint of HarperCollins*Publishers*

INCLUSIFY. Copyright © 2020 by Stefanie K. Johnson. All rights reserved. Printed
in the United States of America. No part of this book may be used or reproduced
in any manner whatsoever without written permission except in the case of brief
quotations embodied in critical articles and reviews. For information, address
HarperCollins Publishers, 195 Broadway, New York, NY 10007.

HarperCollins books may be purchased for educational, business, or sales
promotional use. For information, please email the Special Markets Department
at SPsales@harpercollins.com.

FIRST EDITION

Designed by Bonni Leon-Berman

Library of Congress Cataloging-in-Publication Data has been applied for.
ISBN 978-0-06-294727-7

20 21 22 23 24   LSC   10 9 8 7 6 5 4 3 2 1

To the loves of my life, Piet, Katy, and Kyle Johnson.
I hope you create and enjoy a more Inclusifyed world.

CONTENTS

INTRODUCTION

Another day, another corporate cafeteria. The setting was typical, the actors were the same, even the costumes were typecast: large beige building with lots of free snacks and high-performance beverages; the human resources (HR) specialist in her blue skirt suit, me in black heels, black pants, and a jaunty jacket. But there was something a little different about that day back in July 2016.

I was interviewing top-level executives and subordinates at a Fortune 100 company to learn how the best leaders get results while leading in a diverse environment, part of my research at the Leeds School of Business at the University of Colorado Boulder. I had just taken an all-day flight to New York after doing some work in the Netherlands, so I wasn't sure if my jet-lagged brain was firing on all cylinders.

As I entered the cafeteria, I tried to listen intently to the HR specialist who was filling the dead air with details about all of the new programs the company was running: pulse surveys, mentorship programs, leader training, job rotations.

But in that moment, I was preoccupied with one of my meetings earlier that day. I had interviewed an executive, Jim, who had said impressive things about his approach to leading in a diverse environment. He had seemed great. But then I had interviewed a member of his team, Tawny, who had told me a whole different story. "I'm asked for my opinion, but in the end my opinion never matters," she'd said. It made me wonder: Was Jim a bad leader? Was Tawny an underperforming employee who liked to complain? Or was it a bit of both? Clearly, there was a disconnect. I wanted to know more.

As I paid for my sandwich and bag of Doritos, the musical sound of a multitude of different languages caught my ear. Looking around, I found myself in a room filled with people of all different ages, races, and genders. I was not at all surprised at the diversity of the crowd—we live in a diverse world, and this was a global company based in New York. But what stood out to me that day, even though I had seen it many times before, was that most people were seated in homogeneous groups. There were a table of Asian Americans, a table of young white women, a table of Latinos, a table of old white guys, a table of young white guys.

It made me wonder: If we are all segregating around the lunch table, do we do the same around the conference table? I knew that when it comes to starting companies, women, people of color (POC), and women of color (WOC) are more likely to start teams together.[1]

Likewise, venture capitalists are more likely to partner with founders who share the same background. But they do so at their own peril. For example, a group of venture capitalists is 25 percent less likely to invest successfully when all members are of the same race than when there is diversity on the team. Why? Because they are missing out on different perspectives. We see the same negative effects in homogeneously educated groups: venture capital teams are 18 percent less successful when they invest with another venture capitalist who graduated from the same alma mater.[2]

So if the lunch table behavior I was witnessing extended to the meeting table, this organization's teams were probably not performing as well as they could. It might also help to explain the confusing interviews I'd just conducted with Tawny and Jim. In fact, it might explain why, in general, most corporate diversity efforts fail.

I thought Jim had said all the right things about leadership during our conversation. But Tawny's experiences did not jibe with her boss's words. I felt as though she was talking about a completely different person than the one I had met. It was classic "he said, she said."

HE SAID: "I really like people to try new things. That is how we innovate."

SHE SAID: "Let's just say, if someone's new idea doesn't work, there will be consequences."

HE SAID: "I am all about empowerment—I like to let people do things their own way."

SHE SAID: "We really get no guidance at all. He calls it 'empowerment,' but I just feel lost."

HE SAID: "I always ask for everyone's input on decisions. But at the end of the day, it is my job to decide."

SHE SAID: "I am allowed to be in the room and give my opinion, but I'm not really included because in the end my opinion never matters."

Tawny wasn't done. She added that her performance wasn't recognized. She told me that she'd landed a large client, yet Jim had never even mentioned it. She also complained that she did not feel like part of the team. "In fact," she said, "there is no team, just a bunch of people trying to outperform each other to please Jim. But we're all on our own. It feels like *The Hunger Games*."

As a result, Tawny, like so many others in the United States today, was not engaged in her work; she was just going through the motions to get through each day and was no longer taking on new challenges. It weighed on her that we spend the majority of our waking lives at work, and she'd had enough. She had decided it was time to look for a new job.

For the last fifteen years, I have been studying the intersection of leadership and diversity: how teams perceive female and minority leaders and what leaders can do to increase the variety of race, ethnicity, experience, background, and perspective in their workforce. In that time, despite the notable increase in companies making diversity a priority and implementing diversity programs, the Fortune 500 has not made much progress. There is still a dearth of women, POC, WOC, and LGBTQ in the top ranks of organizations. As of 2019, women and POC comprise only 25 percent and 27 percent of executives, respectively. Only 5 percent of CEOs are women. *Five percent!* This is despite the fact that women make up 51 percent of the population and minorities make up 39 percent of the population. For example, 13 percent of the population—but fewer than 1 percent of Fortune 500 CEOs—is black.

Even at companies that try hard to recruit women, POC, WOC, and LGBTQ, leaders report that the diversity management efforts are not working. In April 2016, I spoke at the White House summit on diversity in corporate America to an audience of Fortune 500 chief executive officers, chief diversity officers, and other thought leaders. Our conversations made it clear that they, too, were struggling to get the most out of their diversity efforts. Their teams weren't bonding, their employees' engagement was low, and some employees felt excluded.

After meeting Tawny, I became curious to learn more about what leaders could do to fully harness the power of diverse perspectives and ensure that they keep their talented employees and attract new ones. It's not just CEOs who need to solve this problem. CEOs may change policy, but it is the managers throughout the organization who have the strongest impact on teams. I went on a quest to understand why some leaders are able to attract, retain, and engage diverse teams while others miss opportunities or fail altogether. I read the research, conducted laboratory experiments, did field studies with a multitude of organizations, and interviewed more than a hundred leaders and followers, including the CEOs of major corporations who were getting it right, according to their employees and profit-and-loss reports, and leaders at all levels who were getting it wrong. I uncovered the two skills that the best leaders had in common.

First, they embrace different perspectives and backgrounds. Second, they fit all the unique pieces together to create a cohesive, interdependent team with a shared purpose. Together, this set of behaviors enables people to do what I call *Inclusify*. Unlike "diversifying" or "including," Inclusifying implies a continuous, sustained effort toward helping diverse teams feel engaged, empowered, accepted, and valued. And although few people are born Inclusifyers, there are specific steps that leaders can take to become one.

In·clu·si·fy	To live and lead in a way that recognizes and celebrates unique and
/in ˈkloōsə/fī	dissenting perspectives while creating a collaborative and open-
Verb	minded environment where everyone feels they truly belong.

Some leaders say, "I don't see why *I* should have to change *my* behaviors so others can feel comfortable." Fair enough. You don't have to. But you should want to. If I offered some tidbit of advice that was sure to increase sales, drive innovation, or reduce turnover, wouldn't you want to do it? Inclusifying achieves all of that and more. And it is not painful. Racism, sexism, harassment—those things are painful. Creating a diverse, inclusive workplace can make your work more enjoyable.

My goal is to share the lessons I have learned that can help leaders understand *why* their current approach to diversifying their workforce may not be working and *what* they can do about it. None of the bottom-line benefits of diversity has to come at the cost of happy employees. Leaders who Inclusify will have better relationships with their teams, elicit greater productivity from all of their workers, and create a more positive environment for everyone. Inclusifying can change a company by making it possible for unique perspectives to be heard, thus allowing the best, most innovative, and creative solutions to emerge while creating an atmosphere in which all employees can be truly engaged.

Engagement is paramount to a successful business. It is a key driver of performance, with the most highly engaged workers outperforming others by 10 percent in customer ratings, 21 percent in productivity, and 22 percent in profitability.[3] Overall, companies with highly engaged workforces outperform their peers by 147 percent.

Inclusifying is the leadership skill of tomorrow, but you can capitalize on it today. It starts with understanding the two most basic human drives: to be unique and to belong. In other words, we want both to stand out and to fit in; to be singularly ourselves but also to be part of the collective We. I did not invent this concept; psychologists have long recognized that we strive to balance these fundamental human desires.[4] And it has been theorized that achieving these needs is essential for employees to experience inclusion at work.[5] Yet what I noticed is that most of the leaders I interviewed underestimated the importance of helping their team members feel as though they belong or miscalculated the importance of celebrating their team members' uniqueness.

Luckily, there are ways that leaders can create an environment that allows their team members to meet both of these fundamentals. For employees to feel like themselves, leaders need to embrace their team members' differences and highlight the benefits of listening to varied perspectives. For followers to feel that they belong, leaders need to show every team member that he or she is a valued, essential piece of a larger group with an important mission.

Of course, these two ingredients have an inherent tension: being your unique self is easy if you don't have to interact with people who are different from you, and creating a team is straightforward if everyone on the team is the same. Because of this tension, most leaders miss out on one or the other of these two ingredients and end up with either cohesive teams of people who all act similarly or a lot of diverse individuals who don't gel.

More than once as I conducted my research, I would be talking to a leader and suddenly feel a sense of dejà vu. Everything they said would seem eerily familiar, and their style would remind me of someone else. Later, I would go back to my notes and find that many leaders I'd interviewed had expressed themselves similarly. They shared common challenges because they weren't focusing on one of the two key human needs—they were not adequately allowing people to be themselves, or they were unsuccessful in making people feel as though they belonged.

Over time, my interviews began to reveal six specific archetypes, falling along two axes (see the chart on next page). Leaders who underestimated the importance of the team often had employees who did not feel that they belonged; leaders who ignored the benefits of listening to different perspectives left some people feeling that they could not be their unique selves.

Some leaders did neither. Others did both minimally and had not yet fully committed to embracing and implementing either. As I heard more and more stories, I concluded that most leaders fall into one of these four buckets, which I call the "Four Follies," that keep them from getting the most out of their teams. These follies are: missing out on uniqueness, missing out on belonging, missing out on both, and not fully committing to either. Those who avoided the follies hit the sweet spot that made them Inclusifyers.

Inclusifyers had realized the importance of both these essential human drives and therefore were able to get the most out of their diverse teams. Interestingly, the mistakes that leaders made were often similar. For example, two leaders from very different companies, industries, and professions would ground their leadership philosophy in the belief that "the strongest players win" and use identical language about wanting to "hire the best person for the job." But as I'll explain, it's a myth that the strongest always win, as is the idea that there is ever a "best" person for a job, and leaders and managers who rely on these unfounded beliefs to direct their hiring, firing, and promotions actually hurt their business. The people I met were rarely ill intentioned; they just really believed in the myths they had been taught.

Interestingly, the myths and mistakes that were common for white men to believe differed slightly from those that impeded women and people of color and led two of the archetypes to manifest differently. Altogether, there are six archetypes highlighting the subtle ways in which leaders miss out on uniqueness and belonging:

Meritocracy Manager: Wants to hire the "best people for the job" but does little to appreciate the unique qualities of his employees or help them feel that they belong to the same team.

Culture Crusader: Focuses on creating a team of like-minded people and ends up forgoing the benefits of incorporating different thoughts, perspectives, and backgrounds.

Team Player: A subset of Culture Crusaders (mostly women, POC, WOC, and LGBTQ) who work so hard to assimilate with the group that they lose touch with the value their own and others' diverse perspectives add to the team dynamic.

White Knight: Takes a paternalistic approach to women, POC, WOC, and LGBTQ and tries to "save" them. The resulting lack of emphasis on shared goals diminishes team cohesion because people cannot see how they fit together.

Shepherd: A subset of White Knights, Shepherds are women, POC, WOC, and LGBTQ who offer in-group support but in doing so cause people to question their motives, resulting in a less cohesive team.

Optimist: Sees value in uniqueness and belonging but is not committed to actively creating change and so maintains the status quo through inertia.

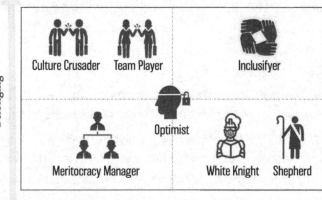

If you want to take a test to find out your scores on the Inclusify matrix, please text "matrix" to 844-476-9863 and the automated service will share the survey with you.

Further, I learned lessons from what I gleaned during my interviews with business leaders and have translated them here so that anyone can learn to be an Inclusifyer. My interviews revealed eight key behaviors exhibited by Inclusifying leaders. Four of them focus on supporting uniqueness (or the SELF) and four of them focus on enhancing belonging (or the TEAM). Throughout this book we'll explore these concepts in depth.

To encourage uniqueness:
• **Support:** Inclusifyers publicly support diversity. They do not pretend to ignore difference; instead, they recognize and embrace it.
• **Empathize:** Inclusifyers get to know their people so they can begin to understand the needs of their team members.
• **Learn:** Inclusifyers have a hunger to learn from others' unique perspectives and try to hire people with diverging opinions and bring out different perspectives within existing talent.
• **(Be) Fair:** Inclusifyers see that it is essential for employees to feel that they are treated fairly. This means reaching not only equality but also equity by giving people what they need to be successful.

To create belongingness:
• **(Be) Transparent:** Inclusifyers are aggressively transparent about their practices, so people know how things work in the organization and understand how they appear to others.
• **Empower:** Inclusifyers empower team members to make their own decisions, conveying high expectations for success.

- **Align:** Inclusifyers actively work to align allies into the diversity and inclusion conversation.
- **Motivate:** Inclusifyers motivate their teams by building spirit and infusing diversity, inclusion, and belonging into the organization's values.

We'll hear about well-meaning leaders who fell prey to one of the Four Follies with unexpected consequences that undermined their teams, resulting in a lack of inclusion. We'll explore how to recognize the myths and misperceptions that drive these behaviors, and I'll give you practical road maps and strategies for you to become an Inclusifyer. By learning why uniqueness and belonging are so imperative to their employees, leaders can better understand what makes their followers tick and find ways to encourage all of them to be themselves while ensuring that they also feel like part of the team. The end result is a fully engaged organization filled with diverse perspectives that create innovative and creative ideas that drive value.

In Chapter 1, I will introduce the concepts of uniqueness and belonging and why they are so important. Chapter 2 focuses on how our expectations of and learned associations about different racial and gender groups limit our ability to Inclusify. Most of the time these associations are subconscious and unintentional—what psychologists call unconscious biases. Although these biases are not malicious, they shape our behavior patterns and often form the basis of the myths and misperceptions that are at the root of the Four Follies. Chapter 3 describes the path to Inclusifying and highlights three essential lessons that all Inclusifyers need to know.

The following chapters cover each of the archetypes by describing what they are, what behaviors they comprise, and how well-intentioned leaders can pivot to become Inclusifyers. In the last chapter you can read my Inclusify journey. More resources and downloads are available at DrStefJohnson.com, and you can take the quiz to find out which of the Four Follies you are most likely to fall prey to at Inclusifyer.com.

We hear from a lot of CEOs in this book. But Inclusifying is for everyone, not just CEOs. In fact, it is actually more important for middle managers. Only 52 percent of organizations believe their board members are engaged in diversity and inclusion initiatives, and just 39 percent agree that their middle managers are engaged.[6] In writing about those middle managers, I have changed their names to protect their privacy.

My hope is to help you maximize the benefits of diversity and get the most out of your team, whether you're a regional sales manager or a chief marketing officer. My mission is to help you examine your behaviors through a stronger lens than the one most of us have used until now, so the path to Inclusifying becomes clear. We all have the desire to be ourselves while being part of a team. In a competitive talent market in which engagement drives retention *and* profits, Inclusifying is the key to innovation, growth, and continued success.

INCLUSIFY

Chapter 1

THE POWER OF UNIQUENESS AND BELONGING

I feel that when I'm here, I can be myself. I can be loud because it is too damn quiet. But when I voice my opinion, I expect the staff to push back, because I'm not always right. Then we sit down for lunch, and it feels like family dinner where we can all connect.
 —*JANE, MANUFACTURING ENGINEER*

The need to belong is so innately human that no one can deny its importance. On some level we all want to be accepted by others— so much so that social exclusion causes the same areas of your brain to light up that physical pain does.[1] Think of a time when you felt that you did not belong—when you were unwelcomed, unloved, treated with suspicion, or even ignored. How did it feel? If not painful, it was most likely not a situation you would want to find yourself in again. This is part of the reason we try to hire people who are "culture fits" with our organizations. We want to avoid having people who are unhappy or quit because they don't fit in. But only hiring people who fit in limits the diversity of perspective needed to drive innovation. The alternative is to create an inclusive space where people—all of whom are different from one another—can fit together.

Because, just as much as we want to belong, we all want to be our authentic selves. Can you recall a time when you felt like you couldn't be yourself? Maybe you have been in a situation where the other people in the room all held beliefs that were very different from your own and you decided to bite your lip to avoid sharing an unpopular viewpoint. Faking who we are to fit in is exhausting and we all feel most at ease when we can just be ourselves. Even more to the point, we want to know that our unique talents are valued and that our voice is heard and respected. When we feel that these two drives—uniqueness and belonging—are in balance, we feel included. The leaders who create space for their teams to experience that synergy are Inclusifyers.

WHERE EVERYONE KNOWS YOUR NAME: BELONGING

Everyone feels like an outsider every now and again. Think of a time when you walked into a room where there was a social gathering of the opposite sex; imagine walking in on an all-men's cigar party or poker game if you are a woman or imagine walking in on an all-women's baby shower or book club if you are a man (please excuse the stereotypical gender norms). Or think about how odd it might feel to be the one white person sitting at a dinner with a group of black, Asian, Middle Eastern, or Latino people. Or consider how it feels or would feel to be the only straight person at a gay bar. Women, POC, WOC, and LGBTQ people experience this all the time in the workplace. I am no stranger to that feeling. As a female professor in a top business school, I am often the only woman in the meeting room. For some time, I was the only woman in my department (and definitely the only Latina).

When I first joined Leeds I remember routinely tottering up four flights of stairs, in four-inch heels, to get to my office. Boulder, Colorado, is very health conscious, and I wanted to fit in, but deep down I am a girl from LA who loves shoes and fashion. One day, I exited the stairwell and heard two of my male colleagues chatting about an upcoming happy hour. Eavesdropping on the conversation, I stepped a little closer. Awkwardly, I interjected, "Hey, are you guys doing a happy hour?" My voice cracked a little.

Silence. They stared at each other. "Oh . . . uh . . . we didn't think you'd want to go. It's a sports bar—they only serve beer." Okay, they were right. I did not want to go. But I did want to be invited. Not being invited made me feel as though I was not part of the group. More distressing than being left out, however, was the realization that their idea of having a good time was so different from mine. It made me realize that I didn't fit in, so even if they had invited me, I felt, I would not have been able to be myself with them.

I hear a lot of stories of people who feel as though they don't fit in or feel excluded. I met a dapper asset manager at a conference for the National Association of Securities Professionals named Jay. Jay described himself as not being the typical finance guy because he was black and from the South, whereas the financial sector is dominated by white men. He explained that there is a different communication style among East Coast finance guys compared to people he was used to communicating with—mostly other black men and women in the South. When he first started in his New York firm, he was confused about why his coworkers were always laughing. Someone would make a statement about the Hamptons or a restaurant, and everyone would laugh. "What is so funny?" he would wonder. After some time he came to realize that it was just a cultural norm.

One of the toughest settings for him was big conferences where he was supposed to network. "I did not know a lot of people, and I felt like every time I tried to join a conversation everyone would stop talking and look uncomfortable." But one year, he was invited to an after-hours get-together in some bigwig's hotel room. "I thought I was looking good—I was wearing a black suit and tie." When he arrived, at the room, he nervously rang the bell. He thought, "What kind of hotel room has a bell?" "The bigwig opened the door, took one look at me, and said, 'Oh, sorry, are we being too loud?'" Jay stammered, "No, no—not at all. I, uh—I—" "Just kidding," said the bigwig. "I called downstairs, we won't be needing anything tonight." Jay's face felt hot. The bigwig thought that he was hotel staff. "Of course, I left. I was not going to explain who I was. And the next day, I did not even go back to the conference out of fear that I would see this guy and he would realize his mistake." Even though Jay felt as though he should belong, it was clear that to the bigwig and maybe to other conference attendees, he looked more like a staff member than a colleague.

Being mistaken for someone of lower status makes you feel as though you don't belong in your high-status group; this phenomenon happens to women, POC, and WOC all the time. For example, one study of lawyers showed that 57 percent of women of color and 50 percent of women have been mistaken for non-lawyers including custodial staff, administrative staff, and court personnel—a phenomenon experienced by only 7 percent of white male lawyers. I, too, had this experience when I was asked to leave a faculty meeting because my colleague did not know I was a professor.

It was a Friday, and I was having one of those mommy mornings where I was trying to get into my smartest suit and full hair and makeup in under five minutes flat because I had kid stuff to do. But of course between milk and baby food and teeth brushing, I ruined my outfit. Outfit number two, deodorant marks. Drat. Number three: a black dress, blazer, and boots. Perfection. I was trying to look my professional best for a faculty meeting, which feels silly in retrospect but felt overwhelmingly important at the time.

I dashed into the building a little later than I would have liked because of all the outfit switching and darted up the stairs. I waltzed into the conference room, made eye contact with a couple of people, said hello, and started to sit. Before my tush hit the seat, the person running the meeting stammered, "St-Stefanie, you can't be in this meeting. You have to go." I felt my face flush. Was the meeting only for tenured faculty (I was an assistant— meaning pretenured—professor at the time)? I looked around and saw other pretenured faculty. I tried to figure out what was going on but thought I should probably get out of there as fast as I could. I felt like a child who had just gotten in trouble. Even if I could have convinced him that I belonged there, it would have been too embarrassing to bear. Now, to be sure, if this were to happen to-day, I would ask for clarification as to why I should not be there. But that day, in my young self-conscious state, I simply scampered out of the room.

When I got to my office, my heart was beating in my throat. I closed my door and tried to catch my breath. A couple of minutes later, I heard *bap, bap, bap* on my door. I yelped, "Yes," and got up to open the door. There was my colleague. Still stammering, he apologized and explained that he had mistaken me for an instruc-tor and it was a meeting for tenure-track faculty. There is a social hierarchy in academia. Research, or "tenure-track," faculty are the high-status bunch, and teaching faculty are lower status in terms of both pay and workload because they teach more and don't produce research. In my department, there were few women on the research faculty, but the majority of teaching faculty were women.

The colleague said he had realized his mistake as soon as I had left the room. I imagine that someone else had pointed it out. The worst part was experiencing the feeling that Jay, the dapper asset manager, was trying to avoid by skipping the conference the next day. I had to face the person who had just excluded me—not to mention all of my colleagues, who winced and made the awkward "sorry about that" face.

It was an easy mistake to make. When there are few female professors but lots of female teaching faculty, if you meet a woman, she is more likely to be teaching faculty than a professor. It is a probability issue. But the message that I heard, as much as I tried to deafen myself to it, was that I was perceived as low status by those around me. And that is the message that women, POC, WOC, and LGBTQ often hear when they are mistaken for the help, for secretaries, or for spouses of "real" employees.

These types of interactions are often meaningless to the person doing the excluding, but across research studies, subtle and often unintentional jabs like mistaking someone as being in a lower-status position or calling them by another person of color's name (often called microaggressions) have the same effects as, if not worse effects than, blatant discrimination on outcomes such as job performance, turnover, and mental health.[2]

On the flip side, feeling as though you belong creates an entirely different perspective. How do you feel when you really belong to a group that you care about? What is the result of that feeling? The thing about leaders is that they have the power to ensure that people are not left out—the power to create space for everyone to be welcomed and be a part of the team *even if they are different*. That's how leaders create belonging, by welcoming people to fit in while supporting them in their desire to stand out.

SHINE BRIGHT LIKE A DIAMOND: UNIQUENESS

At the same time as we want to belong, we all have the desire to be unique. Individualism is essential to the American spirit. We want to know that our unique talents are valued and that our voice is heard and respected. We want to be ourselves and have others welcome us because of who we are. Would it be possible to make myself look more professorial? Maybe wear elbow patches? Or dye my hair gray? Could Jay, the financial analyst from the South, learn to speak Yuppie and laugh at jokes about the local country club? Of course, but if you have been a certain way your whole life, why would you want to change it? It is part of who you are, and changing it seems to imply that your way is somehow less. If I tried to look more professorial I would feel less authentic and less confident. I want to be accepted as myself. And my research shows that most people feel the same.

The struggle over how to be ourselves and still fit in has affected teens and young adults for generations, though the desire to be one's true self is especially strong among millennials and Gen Zers who have been told their entire lives to "be yourself" and "do you." I remember an Asian American girl I grew up with in Alhambra, California, named Tran. She changed her name to Alice—many Asian Americans in my community changed their names to sound more Caucasian. But Alice is a common name, so over the years she changed it to Allis, Allyce (pronounced al-*eese*), and Allie. She wanted to be unique just as much as she wanted to fit in.

We all willingly give up tiny bits of ourselves—at least on a temporary basis—every day. But then there are elements of ourselves that we resist abandoning, even for a moment. Those are the characteristics that make up our identity—the way we want to see ourselves and want to be seen by others. For example, if someone asks you, "Who are you?" or says, "Tell me about yourself," the attributes that immediately come to mind likely reflect your identity.

For me, the first two aspects of my identity that come to mind are professor and parent. If someone asks me to tell them about myself, I think of these aspects of my identity, depending on the context or situation. I am a business professor who studies the intersection of leadership and diversity. *Or* . . . I am mom to Katy and Kyle, the world's smartest, funniest, most perfect children.

But if you were to dig deeper, other aspects of my identity would emerge. First, I am a Mexican American female. Even though people generally perceive me to be white (which I am, half white) my Hispanic heritage is central to who I am. I am a woman—and I love being a woman. I was raised Catholic and am deeply committed to family. Because these identifiers are such a deeply ingrained and important part of me, I don't want to hide them—even in the workplace. In addition to our personal identities, we have social identities that describe our membership in groups that are salient to us.[3] For example, I might identify with my church group, my work group, my book club, or my university (Go, Buffs!). Of course, everyone has both individual and social identities.

For some people, their race is very central to their identity, whereas for others, it may not be as important but their gender or sexual orientation might be particularly important. Furthermore, in one of the greatest advances in gender and identity theory over the last fifty years, Kimberlé Crenshaw developed the idea of intersectionality, pointing out that you cannot understand one identity (such as being black) without understanding other identities (such as being a woman) so that being a black woman is something different from just the combination of being black and being a woman.[4] Indeed, such intersections greatly affect how we are viewed by others and how we view ourselves.[5] Individuals with intersectional identities are constantly trying to navigate the complexities of fitting in or standing out in multiple competing ways.

Regardless of which aspects or intersections of one's identity are salient, it is difficult for anyone to feel accepted when he or she is forced to hide a central aspect of who he or she is. I've seen the strain that this type of masking can cause in minorities who feel that they have to "act white" and in women who feel that they have to "act like men" to succeed at work. The tension of not feeling like part of the group or not being able to be yourself can create emotional exhaustion and cause you to leave your job.[6]

Although masking is a fairly common practice, no other masking has hit me quite so hard as that of friends in the LGBTQ community who have told me that they had to pretend to be straight or cisgender. My friend Brianna Titone, the first transgender state representative in Colorado, told me how difficult it had been to live an unauthentic life, pretending to be someone society expected her to be. Her friends, family, and community had helped to give her the strength to come out as a woman. It might have helped that she lived in liberal Colorado and surrounded herself with open-minded individuals.

I remember reading about football star Ryan O'Callaghan. He was an offensive tackle for the New England Patriots and the Kansas City Chiefs, and he was gay—a fact he hid from the world, including his closest friends and family, for almost three decades. At six foot seven and 330 pounds, he could certainly pass as a stereotypical straight guy. But he also knew that playing football was a great cover for his homosexuality. So when a shoulder injury threatened to take away his "beard," he turned to prescription pills to numb the pain and eventually hit such a low point that he decided to end his life. All the pretending was finally too much for him.

But the story has a happy end thanks to an Inclusifyer. The Chiefs' general manager, Scott Pioli, had repeatedly sent the message to his players that not only were they a cohesive team— they had to be to thrive on the field—but they were also human beings, loved and respected for who they were as individuals. That, combined with the encouragement of a therapist who suggested he might want to see how people reacted to his news before attempting suicide, might be why O'Callaghan, in an incredibly brave move, came out to Pioli in his office just after the season ended in 2011.

Pioli, a huge advocate for LGBTQ rights and gender equality, was unfazed by O'Callaghan's revelation. In truth, Pioli had been in similar situations with other athletes. He was happy that O'Callaghan trusted him enough to share such personal information with him. "I want to know about people—their real selves," Pioli told me. "Maybe people see that I seem like a safe space to them. So players are willing to share this stuff with me, and I want to be there for them." This small act of Inclusifying was so important that it literally saved O'Callaghan's life by giving him the acceptance he needed to be who he really is.

That is what Inclusifyers do. They don't pretend that they don't see race, gender, or sexual orientation, as many people proudly proclaim. To reinforce uniqueness, pretending race and gender don't matter just does not work; it does not promote the integration of diversity to create greater learning organizations.[7] I heard this message loud and clear when I visited the late CEO of Kaiser

Permanente, Bernard Tyson, in his Oakland office. I asked him what was different about his approach to diversity, and he explained that his approach is to notice and celebrate difference. "We don't pretend, we don't walk around talking about how we're color blind. We don't do that. We face the difficult issues and conversations."

Pretending that we don't see race or gender is actually hurtful to people of color, women of color, and women. First, if you don't see race, for example, what do you see when you meet an Asian person? To me, if you don't see their race it means "I don't view you as less than; I see you as white." But can you see how that is insulting? It suggests that white is the norm and the ideal. Second, seeing everyone as being the same actually denies people their basic human need of uniqueness. I think of my race and gender as something that adds value to the conversation, rather than something that should be ignored. Third, ignoring gender or race denies the fact that someone might have experienced sexism or racism in the past. And to negate those experiences sends the signal that you don't care about that person.

UNIQUENESS + BELONGING = INCLUSION

Without both of these essential ingredients, one cannot feel included. At the worst end, you can imagine feeling that you don't belong and your uniqueness is not seen. This causes employees to feel *invisible*. What does that look like in the workplace? Invisible employees are often shift workers or remote workers, who may actually go unseen by their coworkers. But you may also feel invisible if your job role is discounted by those around you. For example, cleaning staff often go unnoticed in the office. No one makes eye contact with them, no one says hello, and no one ac-knowledges their work. Being totally ignored can cause you to feel dehumanized, to experience shame, and to want to quit your job.[8] But feeling invisible is not limited to support staff. Research stud-ies show that women, POC, and WOC often feel invisible at work, receiving a lack of eye contact from their peers, feeling excluded from social events and work discussions, and being talked over, ignored, or discounted during meetings.[9] In fact, many faculty of color report being mistaken for the cleaning staff.[10] The result of making people feel invisible is lowered well-being, mental health, productivity, and commitment to the job.

You can also imagine feeling that you are accepted, but only when you "cover," or "code switch," to fit in.[11] This causes people to feel *incomplete* because they have a sense that they belong, but only insofar as they are willing to deny their unique identity. In an effort to fit in, individuals might change their appearance, alter their language, and overlook bias from others.[12] But all that faking can limit the extent to which teams benefit from your unique per-spective, can cause you to experience reduced authenticity, and can isolate you from other members of your identity group.[13] We most often think of women, POC, WOC, and LGBTQ individuals hiding aspects of themselves—but really this is a phenomenon that plagues many people with stigmatized identities, or things about ourselves that we hide to avoid being judged or excluded. For example, people might hide the fact that they grew up poor, deny religious beliefs, or obscure a disability. But covering is problematic because sharing information about yourself yields a suite of benefits from mental health to interpersonal connections with others.[14]

On the other hand, some individuals who are recognized for their uniqueness still do not feel included because they are faced with harassment, discrimination, or social isolation as a result of their identity. In this case, you feel *insular*—detached and alone. Hearing people in the halls planning a casual lunch and not being invited, hearing conversations go on around you in meetings while you are not invited in, or having your work accomplishments overlooked in comparison to others shows you that some people belong, but you do not. Individuals can also feel a lack of belonging when they feel tokenized for their identity or pigeonholed as the "diversity person" when that is not the role they have chosen.[15] And it is not only women, POC, WOC, and LGBTQ people who experience this feeling—solo men or whites can also feel insular in cases where they are the ones left out as a result of their race and gender.[16] Engagement and performance suffers, and you might quit to avoid the feeling of isolation you're experiencing.

Contrast these feelings with when you feel *included*: valued and accepted for who you are. You feel that your ideas and contributions are recognized and that you are an essential member of the team. You feel engaged, you work hard, and you want to go to work. This is the goal of leadership: to create inclusion so that employees' work is beneficial to their organization and those employees benefit from working in that organization. Rather than ignoring difference, Inclusifyers create a team where everyone belongs because they know that acknowledging everyone's unique talents and perspectives strengthens the organization. It is really about finding ways to help everyone contribute to the team's goals and feel like a valuable piece of the group. In my research, I have found that most leaders want to achieve these outcomes. They want their group members to feel engaged, supported, and included. They just don't always know exactly how to get there, or they make tiny missteps that impede their success. Usually, these mistakes are the result of myths that obscure their view of the world around us and hold them back.

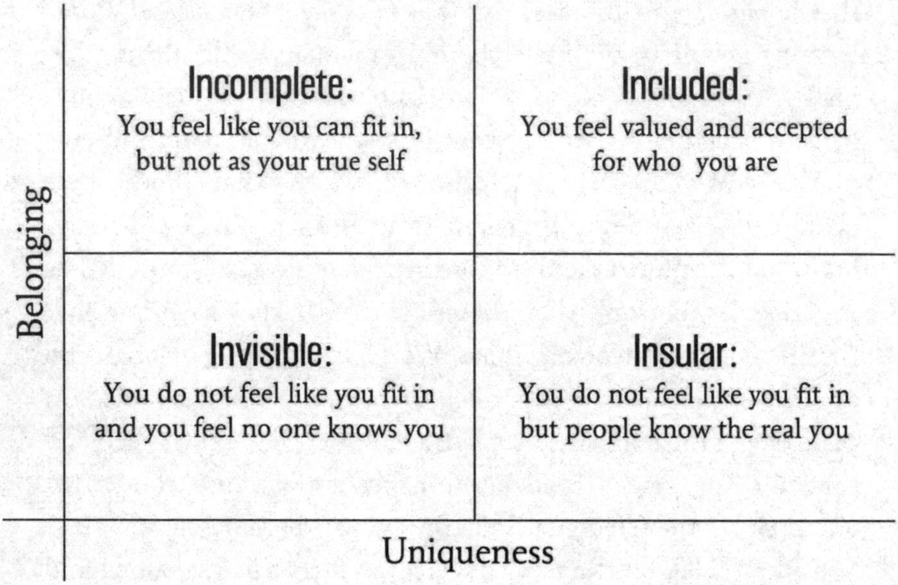

Incomplete: You feel like you can fit in, but not as your true self	**Included:** You feel valued and accepted for who you are
Invisible: You do not feel like you fit in and you feel no one knows you	**Insular:** You do not feel like you fit in but people know the real you

(Vertical axis label: Belonging; Horizontal axis label: Uniqueness)

Chapter 2

THE ABCS OF BREAKING BIAS

People talk about unconscious bias, but it's not like some-body's intentionally discriminating. They're just sticking with like-minded people. Frankly, I don't know how I feel about unconscious bias, because on some level, you are just selecting people like yourself.
—*NONPROFIT LEADER*

Before I learned about Inclusifying, I spent much of my time and my career focused on mitigating unconscious bias. Interrupting unconscious bias can be achieved through the exposure effect—just getting to know people who are different than you. Having a gay friend can make you much more open to LGBTQ rights. Similarly, trying to think of someone as an individual and see things from his or her perspective rather than inferring that he or she embodies all women, POC, WOC, or LGBTQ will reduce bias. Trying to see things from others' perspectives can help as well.

Another approach to reducing bias is to reduce the possibility for bias to occur.

Many of the challenges associated with creating diverse and inclusive organizations come down to unconscious bias (also referred to as *implicit bias*). We have all heard this term in the media and the workplace, but most people I have interacted with (a) have no idea what it is and/or (b) are annoyed by the concept of being accused of bias because there's no way to defend yourself against it (if you say you don't have unconscious bias, it seems to prove that you do because you are unaware of it). But you have it. So do I.

HOW WILL I EVER LEARN ABOUT IT IF IT IS UNCONSCIOUS?

University of Washington social psychologist Anthony G. Greenwald has been largely credited for founding theories of unconscious bias based on his research.[1] He defines unconscious bias as the state of being unaware of how deeply our past experiences color our newly formed impressions. In their book *Blindspot: Hidden Biases of Good People*, Mahzarin R. Banaji and Greenwald explained that we all carry unconscious biases.[2] Unconscious biases are *normal* (we all have them, because we're all human), but that does not make acting on them okay. Instead, we must find ways to interrupt them. Luckily, we can succeed in doing so, by taking a few simple steps.

The first step any leader needs to take to pivot from being a well-intentioned leader to one who is making change is to admit that he or she has unconscious bias. To be fair, all leaders have unconscious bias, which is, simply stated, a mental association that is stored in your mind without your conscious awareness.[3] The reality is that our brains are overloaded with information. The best estimates are that you process 11 million pieces of information in a given second but are conscious of only about forty of them. The rest all occur outside of your awareness, so your brain forms lots of quick, heuristic associations. These unconscious associations are needed for survival; for example, there are a lot of subtle cues we pick up on to help us decide if strangers are friends or foes.

You can differentiate unconscious biases from sexist or racist attitudes in that they usually occur outside of one's conscious awareness and are associative ("nurses are often women") rather than evaluative ("women are incompetent"). They are created by repeatedly pairing two stimuli, similar to classical conditioning (think Pavlov using a metronome while feeding his dogs so many times that just hearing its ticking would cause the dogs to salivate). We build up the same associations with people. So when you think about a teacher, you generally think of a woman. That is really all that unconscious bias is: paired associations in your mind.

WE HAVE UNCONSCIOUS BIASES ABOUT PRETTY MUCH EVERYTHING

When we think of a secretary, we think of a woman. When we think of a CEO, we picture a white man.* Why? Because most secretaries are women and most CEOs are white guys.[4] Only nineteen Fortune 500 companies are headed by minorities, and only twenty-four are

---

* Disclaimer: I use the term "white men" a lot in this book. I don't have anything against white men. I love white men. Some of my best friends growing up were white men. My dad was a white man. My husband is a white man. Even my son is a tiny white man. I love them all; I just don't believe that 90 percent of leadership talent resides in the one-third of the population made up of white men despite the fact that more than 90 percent of CEOs are white men.

headed by women. There are more CEOs named John and David than there are women CEOs. Johns make up 2 percent of the US population and Davids 1 percent. Women are 51 percent of the population but only 4 percent of CEOs. When we see CEOs, more often than not we see white men, so we associate CEOs with white men.[5]

We have associations like this for most categories. I use the following demonstration to show how unconscious biases affect our views. As you read the sentences below, let an image enter your mind and think about what is going on in each sentence.

The *rock star* was unhappy with the amount of alcohol at the party.

What does the sentence mean to you? What image does it invoke in your mind? I picture a man—a skinny man wearing leather pants dancing on a table, shouting, "I need more alcohol!" I see Mick Jagger. Maybe you see someone else. This picture that you see is your prototype of rock star. You use that prototype to interpret the meaning of the sentence. Now read the next one:

The *nun* was unhappy with the amount of alcohol at the party.

Screeching halt. Do you picture something quite different? I see an old woman with her arms crossed in front of her, shaking her head because there is too much alcohol at a party. This is your prototype of a nun. The prototype helps you to interpret and make sense of the sentence. But notice that the sentences are exactly the same even though you have a very different understanding of the scenario. Let's do another:

After weighing all the circumstances, the *CEO* decided to terminate a few employees.

In this case you probably envision a white man making the tough decision to downsize (or rightsize) a company. He is probably wearing a suit. And if your brain works like mine, he is sitting behind a large wooden desk. This probably reflects an image that you have seen in a movie or television series (since most of us do not regularly hang out with CEOs) and is the most easily accessible picture that your brain generates when you think of a CEO. Read the next sentence:

After weighing all the circumstances, the *drug dealer* decided to terminate a few employees.

Oh, no! That sentence probably activated a different prototype, and the meaning of the sentence has changed quite a bit. Now think about it—how many rock stars and CEOs do you know? Yet we all have the same prototypes in our minds. Imagine how strong your prototypes are of women and leaders and minorities, people we all know and associate with daily.

HEY, MOM, YOU JUST GAVE BIRTH TO A STEREOTYPE

Back in 2011, I had the most important experience of my life: I gave birth to a daughter, Katy. Juggling the demands of motherhood and a full-time career was not easy for me, and I had to learn to be more efficient with my time, so I started closing my office door to avoid distractions. One afternoon, I was hunkered down in my office working on a paper about the benefits of setting goals during leader development when my focus was broken by the voice of one of my colleagues in the hall. He was talking to a job candidate and said, "This is Stefanie's office. She just had a baby, so she's not in much anymore." His tone was neither mean nor judgmental. In fact, the person who said it was one of my favorite coworkers.

My coworker interpreted my closed door as evidence that I was not in the office because he assumed, as many probably did, that my priorities had shifted after having a child. There's a reason for that: many moms do stay home with their children. That is an important point about unconscious biases: they are merely associations. Yet most of the time there is some truth in the association. My colleague was not trying to be sexist, but his unconscious bias led him to stereotype me as a mom who wanted to be home with her child instead of a mom who was sitting in her office writing. I have no doubt that my colleague would have been mortified to know how his comment impacted me, because he had always been a huge supporter of mine.

When we are not aware of our biases, we can't correct for them and they can affect our behavior. A woman working for a boss who assumes she wants to be at home with her child is less likely to be chosen for key positions or opportunities. In a shocking coincidence, my husband also had a child on November 3, 2011, the daughter he had always wanted. And he had to balance being a parent and having a full-time career, too. To reduce interruptions at work, he also became more likely to close his office door. But I guarantee you no one ever looked at his closed door and said, "He's probably home with his child."

PROTOTYPES

As an additional way of making sense of the world, our brain stores images of prototypes, which are the most representative example of a concept. When you thought of a rock star, a nun, a CEO, or a drug dealer, the image that came into your mind was your prototype of that category. Why is this important? Prototypes influence how we view other people. As the Nobel laureate Daniel Kahneman described in his book *Thinking, Fast and Slow*, quick, heuristic processing is needed in order to make sense of the world. He suggests that we all have two systems for decision-making: a heuristic, emotional system (System 1) and a more effortful, rational system (System 2). When we are making quick decisions, it is simply easiest to rely on System 1 because we have so much information to contend with. But this fast system makes errors because it is based primarily on cognitive stereotypes.

Pro–White Man Bias

I will return to the CEO example to show how this happens. White men make up 95 percent of CEOs, so when you think of a CEO, you think of a white man. White men also make up only 31 percent of the population. Do you believe that white men make better CEOs than anyone else? Most people will say no, but the reality is that your brain associates leadership and CEOing with white men. If you consider that this is true of most positions of power and you believe in meritocracy (that people achieve success based on their competence), the obvious inference is that white men must be more competent (meritorious) than other members of society are. Therefore, if you are using System 1 thinking, when your company needs a new CEO, you will likely choose another white man.

Due to the fact that most prestigious jobs are dominated by white men, we have ended up with a general belief that white men are the most competent group of people. I will call this pro–white man bias. To some extent, pro–white man bias comes from what we see around us. It is based on the prototypes that tell us how things are. But here's the thing about prototypes: they don't only tell us how things are (describe), they also tell us how things should be (prescribe). Prototypes form the root of one of the most powerful biases we hold: the status quo bias, or the belief the way things *are* is the way they *should be*. The way it has always *been done* is how it *should be done*. So prototypes also tell us how men and women, whites and minorities, heterosexuals and homosexuals, *should be*.

Norm Violations

That's how we come to the conclusion that men are *supposed to be* strong, assertive, and confident.[6] Think of any man you know who does not fit any of those characteristics. What's his name? He is not particularly strong, assertive, or confident. If you are typical, you will probably think of him as effeminate, weak, and inept. Now think of a woman you know who is not strong, assertive, or confident. What's her name? Do you think poorly of her the way you do of the man who lacks the same characteristics? Most people don't. This is because we don't expect that women have to be strong, assertive, or confident to fulfill their gender role. The male gender role requires men to be competent and leaderlike; the female gender role is to be kind, caring, and sensitive. Think Mom, Grandma, a kindergarten teacher, the sweet lady at the bakery.

So what happens when you meet a woman who does not fit these expectations? Go ahead . . . What's her name? And what do you really think of her? Most people characterize women like this as aggressive battle-axes and strongly dislike them because of their gender role violation. Can you think of a man who is not particularly kind, caring, or sensitive? Probably quite a few, yet you probably don't dislike them for it. This is the reason why competent, aggressive female leaders are so quickly denigrated in society. They have committed one of the ultimate crimes—they are gender role violators.

BREAKING BIAS

You're reading this book because you genuinely want to be the best leader you can be. That's where we all need to start—by shining a light on the biases that might be affecting our judgment and leadership strategies. We all hold biases of one kind or another. But only self-examination can help us make this breakthrough. Yes, it might feel a little uncomfortable, and that's okay. We've all heard that being willing to break out of our comfort zones is a good leadership skill. This is the perfect time to start doing it. To start you on the path to overcoming your biases, I have created the ABCs of Breaking Bias: Admit it, Block it, Count it.

Admit It

One of the first things we have to do to break bias is to start by admitting that it exists. It seems like an easy thing to do, but many people cannot do it and are even less likely to admit that they, as good people, can be biased. But the reality is that we all have biases, and when we try to suppress them rather than acknowledge them, they actually have a greater effect on our behavior than they otherwise would. In what the social psychologist Daniel Wegner called the paradoxical effects of thought suppression, he found that when we try not to think about something, we focus on it all the more.[7] Don't believe it? As you continue reading this page, try not to think about a white bear.

In a study designed to examine the benefits of calling out our biases, a job applicant had a fake scar on his face and his inter-viewer was rigged to an eye-tracking machine.[8] The eye tracker showed that the interviewer kept looking at the scar for just a millisecond at a time. The interviewer would look at the scar, then glance away. Look at the scar, look away. You have probably been in a place like this where you really wanted to look at a scar, food stuck in someone's teeth, or a potentially pregnant belly. And the more you tried not to look at it, the more you focused on it incessantly.

Think back to the white bear. Did you think about it? Of course you did. You cannot actually *not* think about something if you try not to—instead, you think about it more.[9] So what happens if we stop avoiding uncomfortable thoughts about race and gender? Well, in the case of the scar study, in one experimental condition the fake applicant acknowledged his scar. "I have a scar," he said at the beginning of the interview. The eye tracker showed that the interviewer looked at the scar once—and then never again. Maybe he was thinking, "No way, I never noticed!" But by giving himself the opportunity to look at it for a second, he stopped focusing on it, processed it, filed the image away, and moved on.

One way that many organizations such as Pricewaterhouse-Coopers (PwC), Facebook, Coca-Cola, and Lockheed Martin try to get their employees to raise their awareness of unconscious bias is through unconscious bias training. In a higher education setting, one institution that implemented unconscious bias training was able to increase the proportion of women faculty hired from 32 to 47 percent.[10] Sometimes it is just getting that small nudge to under-stand and admit that unconscious bias exists that can make all the difference. More and more companies are implementing uncon-scious bias training to improve their diversity efforts. To that end, Tim Ryan, the US chairman of PwC, started the CEO Action for Diversity & Inclusion group, which now comprises over 800 CEOs.

So when we admit that we have biases, that we don't always know how to act around people who are different from us, it might make for some awkward moments. But if we can at least acknowledge these biases, we can move past them. Now stop thinking about the white bear, already.

Block It

Unfortunately, merely admitting that you have bias (i.e., you are human) isn't enough. It can be impossible to overcome by willpower alone. For example, if you have to make a hiring decision, you first have to alter human resources systems (such as how you select people, promote people, find mentors) to ensure that bias cannot continue to affect your judgment. That means setting your criteria in advance, judging people against those criteria (and not creating new criteria), and then making choices on the applicants' qualifications rather than "culture fit" or your "gut."

The easiest way to achieve this is likely by anonymizing assessments (removing the names from applications) so you cannot be biased. The consulting company GapJumpers showed that when traditional screening was used for hiring, 80 percent of the people who made it to the first-round interview were white, male, able-bodied individuals from elite institutions. In anonymized selection, that number dropped to 40 percent.

Based on the power of anonymizing assessments, my own department decided to do an anonymized search when we needed to hire a new professor. We really wanted to hire the best person for the job, but I had just done a study with my postdoc Ksenia Keplinger that showed that when it comes to hiring business professors, the prestige of one's PhD-granting institution helps people get jobs. Everyone wants to hire a business professor who received a PhD from Wharton, Harvard, or Stanford. I suppose you could argue that this is a type of bias—one in favor of prestigious schools. You could argue that it could be either good or bad—if you believe that the school from which you get your doctorate is a signal of future success. But in academia, you're evaluated primarily on your publications in peer-reviewed journals as the metric of success when you go up for your performance evaluations. So you could argue that rather than choosing people based on the prestige of their PhD-granting institution, you should hire them based on their publication record.

But there was another bias as well. The prestige of one's PhD program predicted placement in a top-ranked business school only for male business professors. The publication record, on the other hand, predicted job placements for women. Why would men and women experience different outcomes after graduating from a prestigious school? Since men are already perceived as inherently competent, an additional signal of competence, such as a PhD from an elite institution, confirms that they are exceptionally competent. Because women and ethnic minorities are seen as less competent, the same signal of competence does not convince us that they are the best people for the job. We also need to check their publication record, teaching evaluations, letters of recommendation, looking for some flaw to confirm our feeling that they are not quite good enough. In that way, women, people of color, and women of color are held to a higher standard than are typical white men.

We in the management department of the Leeds School of Business definitely did not think that we were the few amazing people exempt from biases like these, so we decided to anonymize our whole application procedure. We hired a student to enter the stats of each applicant (number of publications, rank of journals, number of conference presentations, and teaching evaluations) into a spreadsheet and created an algorithm for selection. Our final candidate slate was made up of three women and one Asian man. We ended up hiring two of the women. To me, one of the best things about the process is that no one can ever say that we hired the women because of their gender.

Count It

Everyone has heard the statement "What's measured matters," and this is true of diversity.

Of all interventions, setting goals is the most effective action organizations can take to successfully increase their diversity. In my interviews with CEOs from some of the best companies in the United States, including Starbucks and Medtronic, many told me they had set diversity goals.

A necessary first step in this process involves setting benchmarks. To do so, employers need to consider the population they're drawing from. Imagine you are hiring an engineer and you want to increase the selection of women. What is your benchmark? The population? A little more than 50 percent of the US population is women. Or you could say that you are going to benchmark against college graduates; 20 percent of graduating engineers are women. You could also choose the industry average; only 11 percent of practicing engineers are women. Finally, you could look at what industry leaders are doing. Facebook's batch of new engineer hires was 27 percent women. You could benchmark on that. But does using these numbers make sense if you are in Japan? In Oman? No—in Japan only 5 percent of engineers are women, and in Oman 53 percent of engineers are women. The point is, you need to decide what a relevant benchmark is—hopefully you aspire to do better than the status quo—and set your goals accordingly.

Importantly, success when it comes to diversity cannot be achieved only at the entry level; it is essential that diversity be mirrored from the top to the bottom of the organization. Derek Bang, the chief strategy and innovation officer at Crowe, said, "If we look across and say, 'You know, fifty percent of our new hires are women, but only twenty percent of our senior managers are women,' there's something wrong there. Something systemically, we're not doing something right." Data is a powerful place to start focusing in on where the real issues lie and where in a process systemic bias might be coming into play. Then you can consciously get after identifying solutions. The linkage between diversity and innovation is deeply rooted in the firm's strategy. The firm is keenly aware that bringing diverse perspectives and talent to the table ultimately leads to more creativity and innovative ideas.

Bang's point is a good one. A company is not really diverse, nor can it benefit from diversity, if all of the ethnic minorities are clustered at the bottom, top, or middle of the organization. It does not help improve gender parity if all of the women are in human resources and all of the men are in information technology. In other words, looking at the mean level of diversity is not as meaningful as considering the diversity of teams. When there is diversity on a team, you get the benefit of different ideas and perspectives coming together.

In sum, everyone would benefit from the ABCs of Breaking Bias, starting with the first step of admitting that we have unconscious bias and that those around us do as well. With that as our foundation and a couple of tools to address it, we can begin to move forward into Inclusifyer territory.

Chapter 3

THREE LESSONS TO PUT YOU ON THE PATH TO INCLUSIFYING

Diversity and inclusion affect your company's ability to be successful. I don't want to invest in companies that are behind the times. They are at risk of becoming obsolete. That's why it's the right thing to do. It is also just a pure fairness issue for all people to participate fully in our capitalist democracy.
  —*JOHN W. ROGERS JR., CHAIRMAN, CO-CEO, AND CHIEF INVESTMENT OFFICER, ARIEL INVESTMENTS (INCLUSIFYER)*

Few leaders I met started their careers as Inclusifyers. It was usually a journey that required small shifts and profound experiences before they became full-on Inclusifyers. The ideal prototype of an Inclusifyer, to me, is Marc Benioff, the co-CEO of the billion-dollar tech company Salesforce and author of the book *Trailblazer: The Power of Business as the Greatest Platform for Change.*[1] But before he hit the streets with other Salesforce employees in the 2017 Women's March, he had to go on his own Inclusifyer journey.

I met Benioff at a conference hosted by Billie Jean King as part of the Billie Jean King Leadership Initiative (BJKLI). I was there as a panelist to explain that we can make the business case for diversity all we want, but if we cannot reach people's hearts and make diversity relevant to them, it is going to be difficult to convince them that behavior change is needed.

Benioff was being honored as an ally for his support of women at Salesforce. I was fascinated when I heard his impassioned speech about why he felt equality was so important. I wanted to know—what had grabbed his heart to make him an Inclusifyer? I asked him if I could interview him as part of my research the next time I was out in the Bay Area. A couple of months later I was sitting in his office, and amid the hustle and bustle of meetings around us, he recounted his path to becoming an Inclusifyer.

Benioff always believed in the importance of belonging as a cultural imperative but had not thought about all of the ways that institutional biases and personal differences impede belonging for everyone. Obviously, back in 2015, he could see that there were more male than female employees at Salesforce, but that was expected; there are also far fewer female engineers than male engineers in Silicon Valley. However, he also noticed that women were less likely to stay at Salesforce and were not moving into leadership roles to the same extent as men were. One day, during a candid conversation with a female leader, Benioff asked what more he could be doing for women at Salesforce. She responded, "Well, you could pay them equally."

What? That was a surprise. He'd assumed that women at his company were paid equally, but when he dug into the data, he found that they were not. Women at Salesforce were paid less than men, despite their equal performance. That was a huge blow to

Benioff. Nearly all people have a need to believe that the world is fair; it's called the just-world hypothesis. The need is so strong that people are more likely to blame victims for their fate than accept that bad things can happen to good people.[2] People are especially likely to derogate victims of injustice when they think that those victims do not have the power to resolve the injustice. But it was Benioff's company. He could actually change things if injustice was present! So he set forward to get it done.

After all, he was trying to create a family, and that meant treating everyone fairly. Not only did he adjust all salaries at Salesforce to ensure equal pay, but he went on a quest to learn more about the other things he didn't know about employees' experiences at Salesforce.

He talked with people from different ethnic and cultural backgrounds, attended Ohana group meetings (Salesforce's term for employee resource group meetings), and tried to increase his understanding of unconscious bias by reading the latest research on the topic. Over time, those conscious actions, such as trying to understand how others might experience daily life at Salesforce, unconsciously led him to Inclusify. Now it's natural—every decision he makes focuses on bringing people together. He explains that equality is contagious. If you believe in equality for women, how can you not do the same for people of color, those with disabilities, or individuals from the LGBTQ community?

Thanks to the value the company places on appreciating unique contributions and on creating belonging, Salesforce is consistently voted one of the most innovative companies in the United States, as well as one of the best places to work, and Benioff rates among the top CEOs. The company has also achieved astronomical growth (30 percent a year) with a 2019 fiscal year forecast of $13.1 billion in revenue.[3]

THE PATH TO INCLUSIFYING

Just as Benioff had to face the reality that unconscious bias was influencing women's pay before he could successfully implement change at Salesforce, most of the Inclusifyers I met had to go through a process of recognizing their own unconscious biases so that they became conscious. Once we're aware of our biases, we can overcome them if we choose to do so. Then they started on the path to make structural changes to their organizations to ensure equity and diversity. Although Inclusifying is a continuous process, many leaders had a similar experience as Benioff.

Their general path to becoming an Inclusifyer looked something like this: they had to become cognizant of their unconscious bias, change their behavior when the bias became conscious, and work to engage in Inclusifying behavior. After a while, Inclusifying just became second nature and they did not even have to think about it. It just became their way of being.

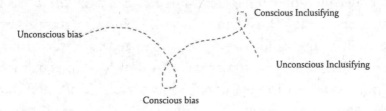

FROM UNCONSCIOUS BIAS TO CONSCIOUS BIAS

The previous chapter discussed unconscious bias and how you can break it. The next step is to move to conscious bias. Now, that does not mean being consciously biased against people; instead, it focuses on an increased awareness of the unconscious biases we hold so that they cannot affect our behavior in conjunction with an awareness of how systems can be biased against certain people.

Three Lessons You Need to Know

There are three foundational points to remember before Inclusifying: First, the playing field is not level; people have to travel different distances to get to the same place. Second, entrenched systems can inhibit your diversity and inclusion efforts. And third, we are living in a post-#MeToo world.

Lesson 1: The playing field is not level.

Even if you have always believed that everyone starts on a level playing field, the college admissions bribery scandal of 2019, in which wealthy parents were caught paying thousands of dollars to exam proctors to change their students' SAT scores or having created fake athletic profiles and paid coaches to accept their kids on university teams to ensure admission, proved that some people are achieving more by doing less.

Many people insist that it is easy to ignore people's background information or argue that it is unfair to hold candidates' relative advantages against them when making hiring or promotion decisions. But I argue that this is a red herring. Even if you don't care about social justice and improving inequality, your organization will be better off hiring people who have achieved more with less because they demonstrate a wealth of skills that will serve your organization.

Dolly Chugh's book *The Person You Mean to Be: How Good People Fight Bias* makes a great analogy.[4] She compares people's different starting points to flying from New York to Los Angeles or in the other direction. It takes as much as forty minutes longer to go from New York to Los Angeles than the other way around because when a plane is traveling west, it faces headwinds, which slow it down. So in the same amount of time, you might make it only to Denver rather than to Los Angeles. On the way back, however, the plane is pushed by tailwinds, which propel it forward and make progress much quicker. So rather than taking five and a half hours, the same voyage in reverse takes less than five hours.

Los Angeles   Denver   New York

The analogy of flights is easy. You can't argue with physics. But when it comes to people, the forces propelling people forward or pushing them back are much harder to see. Kids who have to pay their own way through college might take longer to finish school, but that says nothing about their intelligence or performance; it just means that they faced headwinds. So when those kids make it from New York to Los Angeles in five hours despite the headwinds, I call them "Jets": they flew faster, harder, and smarter than other kids. They are the type of people I want in my team, my organization, and my life.

One of my undergraduate students at Leeds, Sofia Montoya, was born with a genetic condition that caused her heart to be on the right side of her body and her right hand to be missing one finger. She spent the first six months of her life in the neonatal intensive care unit (NICU). She told me, "I am the only kid from that NICU who is still alive today." She had open-heart surgery as an infant and had additional surgeries to put in a pacemaker. She still has challenges with strenuous activity. It doesn't help that she lives 5,280 feet above sea level.

But the reason Sofia stands out to me is that she is just about one of the smartest kids at Leeds. Why should that be a surprise? Here is an individual born into enormous headwinds, but she earned the same SAT scores and GPA as the other students who got into Leeds. Last year, Sofia paid every penny of her college tuition herself through loans, financial aid, and a job at a local hospital. I can see that with so many headwinds blowing against her, she *had* to be smart to make it to the same endpoint—let's just say Boulder—in the same time as everyone else. She is a Jet, not a plane.

How Do You Capture the Jets?

Now, wouldn't you want someone like that working in your organization? Clearly, the kind of grit Sofia exhibits pays off.[5] She is a national spokesperson for the American Heart Association and spends much of her free time inspiring other young men and women with her story of hard work and perseverance. She recently launched a passion project to promote Jump Rope for Heart, a school fund-raiser in which kids jump rope to raise money for the American Heart Association.

Many of the Inclusifyers I met said that they had started to measure other valuable job skills such as leadership, tenacity, and grit in addition to GPA. They expanded the criteria of merit to include new ideas that might yield people who were different from themselves. These measures are in no way biased against white or male students. They account for the fact that anyone may have overcome a huge obstacle. Maybe the obstacle was an illness or finding a way to improve culture on their college campus. The applicant just needs to demonstrate perseverance.

Companies do the same in interviews by asking people behavioral questions about leadership or overcoming challenges. These things are important, not just for increasing diversity but also because they predict success. The point is that by expanding the narrow definition of merit, you might find some Jets that you would have otherwise missed. And you need to recognize that sometimes people have to take an indirect flight path because of unexpected turbulence, so they might have taken longer or taken a less traditional route to arrive at the same location. But sometimes those people are the best ones for the job.

Feel Your Tailwinds

A simple way to become more attuned to others' headwinds is to reflect on your own tailwinds (your good fortune).[6] People tend not to focus on the things that have helped them get ahead and therefore find it harder to see that everyone might not have had the same good fortune. To be quite honest, I had never spent much time thinking about my tailwinds until I was put on the spot a couple of years ago.

I was giving a talk at a liquor manufacturer, Brown-Forman, when the company's chief diversity officer, Ralph de Chabert, asked me, "Stefanie, what were your tailwinds? What tailwinds do you have?" The question really threw me because I grew up in a single-parent household and we lived in an impoverished neighborhood with poorly performing schools. You usually think of tailwinds as things that make your life easier, and I had never felt that my life was very easy.

Of course I also had tailwinds, but when de Chabert asked me that question in front of a crowd of people, what feelings did I experience? I felt defensive and threatened. I wanted to reject the notion of having advantages to show how much I had accomplished and prove that I had earned everything I have. I was aghast at the possibility that someone would dare suggest that I had had special treatment. I felt angry and vulnerable.

But as I took a step back and saw that I was falling prey to one of the very traps I tell other people about, I sucked in a deep breath and faced the discomfort. I pushed the anger aside and leaned into the vulnerability. What could I imagine might have made my flight path easier?

My Tailwinds
- **I was raised Catholic.** In the United States, being Catholic or Christian makes you the norm. Most people celebrate Christmas. I don't have to sheepishly ask for special holidays from work or explain that I eat only kosher foods.
- **My appearance is pretty normal.** Although I am a couple of standard deviations above normal on height, people never whisper about me for having any major physical disabilities.

I went on:

- No one ever crosses the street to get away from me.
- I don't suffer from PTSD.
- People never think I am a terrorist.

Can I admit that life would have been tougher for me if I had not had some of those tailwinds? For sure. It does not mean I did not work hard or I don't deserve what I have earned; it just helps me understand how other people might have different challenges than I have had. It makes me more empathetic to the experiences of others because I understand that they faced challenges I can't even dream of. And rather than making it all about me and my story, if I stop and think about others' stories, I instantly become more empathetic.[7] Really, anyone can do this, and I will ask you to do it, too. Take a moment to think about your own headwinds and tailwinds. To help you reflect on your experiences, please take the time to write down the things that might have helped you achieve success in the space provided below.

What things in your life might have helped you achieve success?

_____

_____

How might your life have been more difficult had you not had each of these things?

_____

_____

Lesson 2: Systems can create inequality.

The second lesson relates to removing systemic barriers to some groups, often referred to as system biases. These are laws, customs, and practices that contribute to inequities in society. Even if people are totally unbiased, the systems in which they operate can still create bias. There are system biases that make it much more difficult for the poor, as an example, to achieve the American dream.

Poor people often live in neighborhoods with underperforming schools, which means that they receive a worse foundation for getting into college. The ability to attend college is often a benefit received by the wealthy since it's so expensive. Even *applying* to college is expensive! So those who have to pay for their own schooling often have to hold down jobs in addition to completing all of their coursework. Middle-class Americans who may not understand or think about how those experiences affect students make the mistake of thinking that kids who have to pay for college or take longer to matriculate are *less smart* rather than just *less wealthy.*

And for those who make the argument that disadvantaged groups have an easier time getting into college, here are a few statistics.[8] Fewer than 5 percent of students in top universities come from the bottom 20 percent of earners. At Yale, only about 2 percent of students come from families who earn less than $20,000 a year— which is the bottom 20 percent of earners. On the flip side, the median income of a Harvard student's parents is about $170,000 a year. That is the *median.* And it is not just Harvard; 21 percent of Dartmouth students' parents are in the top 1 percent of earners, earning more than $630,000 per year.

Now, when it comes to race, one of the inherent biases against minorities (primarily black and Hispanic people) is that they have less wealth. For every dollar of wealth held by white people in the United States, black families have 5 cents. Hispanic people have 6 cents. Considering that socioeconomic status is the best predictor of future wealth, the reasons for racial disparities in success become very clear.

Rewire the System

In 2014, *Wired* analyzed the top five feeder universities for Microsoft, IBM, Google, Apple, Yahoo, Facebook, and Twitter.[9] Three were elite private (expensive) schools: Stanford, Carnegie Mellon, and MIT. There were also two public schools: UC Berkeley and the University of Washington. And since we know that wealth is strongly related to attending elite schools, it is obvious that recruiting from those schools vastly limits the applicant pool. Companies can easily start hiring from a broader pool of schools.

But systemic biases affect more than just hiring. They can also impact promotion and overall success in the workplace. For example, one organization I worked with required that employees take an expatriate assignment in order to be promoted to the vice president level. That meant they'd be spending at least a year working in another country. The company's own data showed that this requirement was holding many female leaders in the organization back. In addition, leaders hired from outside the company at that level did not always have expat experience, raising the question of whether expat experience was really essential. A simple change such as not requiring an expat assignment or providing greater resources for relocation and integration of expat families could make the system fairer.

Women also face system biases because they're penalized for having children, whereas men are not. Women of color get a double whammy of bias. Susan Wojcicki, the CEO of YouTube, showed how flexibility can improve the retention of women. In many ways, Wojcicki was a part of Google from the beginning, as its founders, Larry Page and Sergey Brin, set up an office in her garage when the company was first starting. But 2014 might have been the best year of her life. The same year she took over as CEO of YouTube, she gave birth to her fifth child. Not only did she set an example for other women in their organization when she took maternity leave, but she worked to increase maternity leave to eighteen weeks. When I interviewed her, she explained that her reason for doing so had been to break down the institutional biases that unfairly affect women by providing longer maternity leave and providing resources for women's employee resource groups.

She said that the number of women who left Google had been cut in half following the changes. *Cut in half!*

Lesson 3: We Live in a Post-#MeToo World

It is impossible to discuss diversity and inclusion in 2020 without acknowledging the powerful impact that the #MeToo movement has had on society. Celebrities like Alyssa Milano, Rose McGowen (author of *Brave*[10]), Ashley Judd, Megyn Kelly, and all of the other women (celebrities or not) who risked attack and criticism by telling their stories have made a more aware and equitable workplace for us all.

In a random and lucky research happenstance, my lab had conducted a large-scale study on sexual harassment at work back in 2016—before the #MeToo movement exploded in 2017. In 2018, we followed up on the original study to explore what has changed.[11] The survey of more than 500 employees from across the United States showed that 66 percent of women reported receiving unwanted sexual attention in the workplace in 2016, whereas that number dropped to 25 percent in 2018. In 2016, 25 percent of women in our study experienced sexual coercion at work, compared with 16 percent in 2018.

We also interviewed a group of women in 2016 and re-interviewed those same women in 2018 to ask them their perceptions about how #MeToo had changed the workplace. They spoke extensively about feeling less shame and more support about their own sexual harassment experiences, highlighting the power of women helping women in the workplace. One woman explained that #MeToo had shifted blame from the harassed to the harassers.

"It used to be like, 'Well, why were you out at two in the morning? You must have just been doing something wrong.' Now I think the public is shifting toward putting the attention where it should be, which is disgust and anger toward the perpetrator." Likewise, our quantitative data showed that sexual harassment was not as damaging to women's self-esteem in 2018 as it was in 2016.

Of course, all of the news is not good news. We also found that women were experiencing backlash at work—93 percent of women reported hostility against them in the workplace in 2018! That number was 76 percent in 2016. The women we interviewed said the same thing: "There's increased hostility toward the women who have been empowered by the #MeToo movement who aren't as quiet about it anymore."

Consistent with our study, several surveys have emerged that outline challenges when it comes to a post-#MeToo world. For example, men report being afraid of false allegations against them and express less desire to mentor women or even be alone with women at work.[12]

So, what does this have to do with Inclusifying? From my view, we need to start healing together and bringing down the barriers between men and women that are creating an us-versus-them mentality. I encourage bystander intervention training to help enlist men as allies against harassment in the workplace. I will also note that the fear that men are experiencing is very real to them, even if the data show that false allegations are extremely rare. In much the same way women need an empathetic ear to listen to our experiences, we need to be empathetic toward the fact that the workplace is changing for men—and change is hard.

#MeToo has also shown us how organizational systems can actually protect predators in the workplace (Ronan Farrow's book *Catch and Kill* does a great job of showing this[13]). HR professionals need to think deeply about how their systems are designed and whether they are truly effective at creating a safe and productive environment for everyone. Being proactive about sexual harassment could save organizations billions of dollars; corporate scandals like those we have seen during #MeToo cost an average $4 billion per company.[14] The psychological cost to those who are harassed is much greater than that. Thus, organizations need to remain vigilant and continue to improve systems and processes.

MOVING TO CONSCIOUS INCLUSIFYING

Once you have confronted your unconscious biases and begun to think about how inequalities can sabotage diversity, it is time to move toward making conscious efforts to Inclusify. In the chapters that follow, I offer the best first steps for leaders of all types to improve their Inclusifying skills. Feel free to mix and match any of these tips and techniques. I will also move through each of the Four Follies that leaders fall prey to and explain how you can pivot to put yourself on the path to Inclusifying.

Chapter 4

MERITOCRACY MANAGER

How Can Merit Be Bad?

I don't care who sits in front of me, if they're black or they're white or they're orange or they're green. I need the smartest person because it only helps me. And I'm very selfish that way.
—SENIOR EXECUTIVE, GLOBAL DISTRIBUTION

MERITOCRACY MANAGER: ORIGINS

As they work to lead and unite their diverse teams, most leaders find it is hard to achieve their goals. You might feel that way, too. You may want to diversify your high-performing team, but you have trouble finding nonwhite men who are up to snuff. Conversely, you may have a diverse team, but the nonwhite members don't seem to be as engaged and high performing as the rest and you are wondering how to motivate them. Either way, you might be feeling that you want to make some changes. The challenge is that you always want to hire the best person for the job and you expect excellence from all of your employees. Essentially, you believe in merit.

Meritocracy Managers hold the ideal of merit above all else and therefore try to hire, promote, and reward based on performance alone. There is nothing wrong with expecting excellence, and most Meritocracy Managers probably believe it was the secret of their own success. They probably grew up as hard workers who saw how their effort translated into success, whether through sports or school or business. If they did not win the championship, they trained harder the next season. If they did not get the A, they hired a tutor and studied more. Does that sound familiar? Could I be describing you?

I get it. I believed in merit, too. As a high school student doing homework into the wee hours of the morning on my black futon with a Super Big Gulp of Mountain Dew by my side, I used that ideal to maintain the motivation to push harder and do better. Like so many people, I idolized self-made billionaires such as Ralph Lauren, Howard Schultz, Oprah Winfrey, and Michael Jordan, because they inspire us to believe that we can be billionaires, too. Success is not out of our reach if we just work harder. And success begets success. Each time we set our goals and worked and sacrificed until we met them, we solidified our belief that if we were smart enough or talented enough and tried hard enough, it would pay off; it became a fact to us. That is the inherent appeal of believing in meritocracy. For me, believing in meritocracy was comforting. Without that belief, why even try? After all, it is the American way.

Who Is the Best Person for the Job?

If you believe in meritocracy, if you believe "I just want to hire the best person for the job" or "I don't want to lower the bar," or that effort times ability equals success or that success is due exclusively to hard work, then other people's lack of success can only mean that they didn't try hard enough. They weren't willing to do what it takes. So it makes sense to hire people with the best credentials. By your definition of merit, it means hiring from a pool of the smartest who have worked the hardest.

But ask yourself this: Isn't it possible that some people end up with the credentials without having done the hard work? The recent college admissions scandals I mentioned earlier, in which high-profile celebrities and other wealthy parents paid a fake non-profit to buy their kids' way into some of the top schools in the country, clearly showed that not all credentials are earned. And if it's possible that some people succeed by methods other than merit, couldn't it also be possible that some people who have tons of merit were unfairly blocked from achieving their goals? Isn't it possible that the system is not totally fair? It may not be intentional, but the subtle decision to ignore the instances when merit fails and luck (or outright cheating) prevails is what leads Meritocracy Managers to justify a lack of diversity and to dismiss injustice as an unfortunate but intractable part of society.

In one study that illustrates the issue, researchers hired confederates (actors who are in on the study) to apply for 340 jobs in New York. The confederates were Latino, black, or white. The experimenters created fake résumés that were all identical in quality. The confederates, who received interview training to standardize their behavior, went for actual job interviews and the experimenters measured their success in obtaining a second interview or job offer. The results were staggering. Black applicants were *half* as likely to receive a callback or job offer, though they were equally as qualified as the white applicants. Furthermore, black and Latino applicants with no criminal records fared no better than white applicants just released from prison.[1] This means that the status loss of just being nonwhite is similar to that of being a convicted criminal. Did merit have anything to do with the white applicants' success over that of the black or Latino applicants? Does the tendency for hiring managers to hold a bias toward white-sounding names point to a truly unsolvable social problem or an easily identifiable instance of bias against Asian-, black-, or Latino-sounding names? It is a rectifiable problem—if we are willing to acknowledge that barriers such as disparities in treatment and unconscious bias can undermine a merit-based system.

THE FOLLY OF THE MERITOCRACY MANAGER

In using an overly narrow definition of merit to try and capture the best talent, Meritocracy Managers frequently miss out on it. Their teams are homogeneous, leaving them with dead zones*—areas where they aren't getting any signal or data—which result in competency gaps. Numerous studies show that crowds, as long as the individuals in them are diverse, can outperform experts when making decisions, a phenomenon called the wisdom of the crowd.[2] The idea is that we all make slight errors in judgment and decision-making. If a crowd is very homogeneous, the errors of its members are likely to be more similar to one another. When their responses are averaged, they are likely to agree on an erroneous answer. That is a dead zone.

* This is the same as the concept of a blind spot in one's rearview mirror, but *dead zone* is a less ableist term. In German they call this a *toter Winkel*—or death angle—because it can cause crashes.

But if the crowd is diverse, the errors of its members are *not correlated*, and thus the average of their responses is likely to approximate the correct response. It is appealing to believe that choosing smart people or those with expertise will yield the best results. But we see the same thing time and time again: at the individual level, being smart is good, but at the team level you benefit more from diversity. Diversity improves decision-making by removing dead zones in your organization.

Don't believe you have any dead zones? Try this experiment. Have you ever noticed the scotoma in your field of vision?

Cover your right eye and look at the *X* below with your left eye. Then move your face closer to (or farther away from) the page until you see the *O* disappear. You can do it the other way as well: cover your left eye and look at the *O*.

O   **X**

There is a spot where you can no longer see the *X*, right? Yet most of us go through life believing that everything we see in front of us is all there is. Now, if we all have a little gap in our vision—called a scotoma—imagine the information we're missing if we have a similar information gap in our organization, the missing data that could exist in our perception of our customers' needs, our competitors' plans, or our own cultural shortcomings.

A Team Is More than the Sum of Its Parts

More to the point, you need to have people with different skills to maximize group effectiveness. The truth is, you can't build a football team with all quarterbacks. I call this the myth of multiplicity—the idea that there is one best type of person and the best team is created when you have a bunch of those people. But imagine a team of all 220-pound quarterbacks when the opposition has 320-pound linebackers. They would be crushed! Even though the quarterback is often the "most valuable" player, diversity creates a more effective team. Similarly, your team cannot create the best product if everyone on it shares 100 percent of the same background and experiences.

If I were going to select a team of students for a case competition, I would not choose the five smartest kids based on a measure of test performance (the best student for the job times five). I might start with the top student but then try to round out the team with people who have different skills; maybe someone who has past case competition experience and another person who is a great writer, another who is a great presenter, and a final person who is a great slide deck creator. The presence of different thought patterns and abilities creates better ways of analyzing data and better presentation outcomes.

If you are a Meritocracy Manager or even have some Meritocracy Manager tendencies, bringing these biases to light can aid you in your ability to create great diverse teams. First, there is evidence that just thinking about meritocracy clouds our decision-making. Add to that the fact that we readily manufacture new standards when assessing people, and it can be difficult to be your best leader self. Fortunately, there are proven ways in which Meritocracy Managers can start to strip away some of the myths and misperceptions that impede them from hiring the best person for the job, much less from Inclusifying.

THE MAIN MYTH AND MISTAKE AT THE HEART OF MERITOCRACY MANAGING

The Myth That Meritocracy Means Majority

It is counterintuitive, but just saying that a company promotes meritocracy makes employees *less* likely to support the *objectively best* person for the job in favor of white men. In an experiment using more than four hundred HR professionals, researchers created identical résumés for two job candidates who were equally qualified. The researchers randomly assigned a male name to one résumé and a female name to the other. In one experimental condition they told participants that the company they were doing the hiring for promoted meritocracy, and in the other they did not. There should have been no gender difference in the ratings. Remember, these HR professionals were looking at the *same* résumés. But what the researchers found was shocking.

They found that when participants evaluated the résumés with meritocracy in mind, they rated the male applicant more positively than they rated the female applicant, despite the fact that the candidates were identical. The results indicate that when you tell people to hire on the basis of meritocracy, they actually favor white men.

When they told individuals that an organization valued meritocracy—rewarding people in accordance with their performance—they responded by *favoring* a male employee over an *equally qualified* female employee. Making a hiring decision based on meritocracy caused them to adopt very unmeritocratic decision-making by giving an unfair advantage to men![3]

INCLUSIFYING ACTION: **Delete the word *meritocracy.***

How can it be that when people tell us to use meritocracy as a guideline, we are actually more likely to make biased decisions? If you believe, even unconsciously, that women, POC, WOC, and LGBTQ are not as competent as white men (we call this pro–white man bias), anytime you hire someone who is not a white man, you will believe that you have lowered the bar or engaged in affirmative action. In fact, experiments show that unless it can be proved beyond a shadow of a doubt that a woman or POC was the best candidate for a job or that a company is firmly against affirmative action, people will infer that any nonwhites or women at the company benefited from affirmative action.

In one study, researchers brought a group of participants into a laboratory. One of the members was selected as a leader. For a third of the groups, the experimenter told the group that the leader had been chosen based on gender and the rest of the groups were told that the leader had been selected based on merit or chance. The interesting part of the study was how the groups reacted to female leaders when they were told she had been selected because of gender.[4] When group members believed that their female leader had been selected because of her gender, they both blamed the female leader for their failures and did not to give her credit for their successes. But here is the problem: other studies show that we almost always assume that women, POC, and WOC were hired because of their race or sex.[5] And it is not just in the laboratory. A study by the Rockefeller Foundation showed that newspaper articles attributed organizational crises to the fault of the CEO 80 percent of the time when the CEO was a woman and only 31 percent of the time when the CEO was a man.[6]

Clearly, we need to find ways to subvert these mental barriers. Changing our language is a good place to start.

DELETE	REPLACE WITH
I believe in meritocracy.	I want someone with a 3.5 GPA.
I am going to hire the best person for the job.	The person needs to have ten years of experience.
I don't want to lower the bar.	The person needs to have international experience.

The important thing is to avoid invoking the nebulous terms of meritocracy, which trigger people to think "white male."

Why Does This Happen?

I saw how Meritocracy Managers' minds work during a presentation I gave on the benefits of gender diversity on corporate boards to a room full of executives. I gave them the data:

- Having more women on the board correlates with higher returns[7] and growth.[8]
- Having more women in the C-suite correlates with greater profitability.[9]
- Having more women in top management correlates with greater profitability.[10]
- Having more women in the organization correlates with greater profitability[11] and higher stock returns.[12]
- The benefits of greater diversity are even greater for race than for gender.[13]
- Women and people of color must have more management experience than their white male counterparts to earn their first spot on a corporate board.[14]

A hand in the front row shot up: white guy, midfifties—prototypical person in this crowd.

"At the end of the day, I appreciate what you're saying, but I believe in meritocracy," he said.

That is the tried-and-true motto of a Meritocracy Manager. What is the underlying belief?

My response: "Totally agree. But how does that relate to hiring more women?"

"I'm just saying, you still have to hire the best person for the job. You don't want to lower the bar."

My response: "Totally agree. But when you read the study I reference showing that women are actually held to higher standards to earn board seats, it seems like you are *raising* the bar for women, which makes no sense."

"Yes, but this is business and you have to do what is right for the business and the shareholders."

My response: "Totally agree. And the data show that the thing that is best for stock prices is having a more gender-diverse board."

Well, then, women must not be applying or all of the qualified women are already on boards or they take time off to have children, because if there were qualified women, there would be more women on boards. Why? Because the best person always wins, and if a woman was the best, we would hire her. (The last sentence is my interpretation of his thought process.)

What I see from Meritocracy Managers, like this one, is that they are not dealing with the possibility that their prototype of who is the "best person for the job" could be wrong. Rather than really comparing candidates or discussing their different strengths, they hold on to clichés that don't require them to actually think about the content of their own beliefs.

The Mistake of Manufacturing Standards

The most important mistake you can make as a Meritocracy Manager is thinking that you can assess merit accurately but are inadvertently *manufacturing standards* that support your unconscious beliefs. We all believe that we are experts in evaluating people and we know talent when we see it. Books such as Malcolm Gladwell's *Blink: The Power of Thinking Without Thinking* tell us that we should go with our gut because we pick up on myriad pieces of information when we judge other people.[15] And yes, our powers of perception are strong. But when it comes to evaluating other people, most of the time, we are drawn to people who remind us of ourselves or fit some prototype. Once we choose the person we like the most, we manufacture standards to justify why he or she is the best candidate.

For example, in one study, researchers described two police officer candidates, Michael and Michelle, as either street smart or book smart.[16] They asked participants:

Who would you hire: a book-smart female officer or a street-smart male officer?

Most people chose the street-smart male officer because police officers need to be street smart. Who would you choose?

Other participants were asked:

Who would you hire: a street-smart female officer or a book-smart male officer?

The results of the study showed that when the male applicant was described as book smart, formal education was perceived to be more important to the job. But when the male candidate was described as street smart, street smarts were deemed more important. Unconsciously, the decision makers want to hire the man, so they reverse engineer the merit argument to fit their implicit choice. Indeed, our brains are extremely talented at making sense of information and filling in the blanks. Try to read the sentence below:

Azamignly, your brnai can raed wrods wouthit a pobelrm evne wehn the ltteers are out of oredr.

S1M1L4RLY, when we have an implicit favorite, our tricky little minds are able to create a multitude of criteria that define "merit" to justify hiring that applicant. And even *we* believe that we chose the person based on merit. As Warren Buffett put it, "What the human being is best at doing is interpreting all new information so that their prior conclusions remain intact." Psychologists call this confirmation bias, but it is essentially the idea that we see what we expect to see.

But there is a simple way to get around this. When you choose to Assess (people) Before Criteria are Defined (A-B-C-D) your mind will usually fill in the blanks for you so that you end up choosing the person who best fits your prototype.

However, if you define the criteria for the right hire *before* evaluating candidates (Define Criteria Before Assessing, or D-C-B-A), you are better able to judge all applicants against the same set of criteria and choose the best candidate for the job. Essentially, you start at the end with what you are looking for and work backward to find it.

INCLUSIFYING ACTION: **Follow the D-C-B-A principle.**

When criteria are set up front, Meritocracy Managers are less likely to defer to their gut and end up making poor decisions.

For example, a hiring manager might decide that the best hire will fill the following criteria:

- Works well in high-pressure situations
- Deals with conflict effectively
- Has successfully led a team
- Is resilient in the face of failure

Now all the manager has to do is evaluate each applicant against the criteria. Why is this so important? The way we interpret information is influenced by our prototype of what we are looking for. It might be that a white male college dropout fits the mold because he is supersmart and edgy but a Hispanic college dropout seems unqualified—he doesn't even have a college degree! A fresh-out-of-college finance whiz is a real catch when he is male yet somehow appears inexperienced when she is female. Establishing criteria before you evaluate people will help you avoid unintentional biases and double standards. Of course, you would also hope that the criteria you use are unbiased, but even if they are biased, you are still better off being consistent.

Chapter 5

LEADERSHIP STRATEGIES FOR MERITOCRACY MANAGERS

This is not rocket science. The more your company mirrors the customer base, the more your company is going to succeed. It is the whole richness of thinking and points of view. That really is the basis for our diversity and inclusion.

—DENNIS GLASS, CEO, LINCOLN FINANCIAL GROUP (INCLUSIFYER)

We have to look only as far as Silicon Valley to see examples of how Meritocracy Managing can go astray but be corrected with a little Inclusifying. Usually it requires new leadership to make massive cultural shifts, meaning companies need to change their CEO.

Chris Wanstrath, a former CEO of GitHub (a social network for software development), is my prototype of a Meritocracy Manager. He and his cofounder were so enchanted by the idea of meritocracy that they commissioned a mat as the centerpiece of GitHub's Oval Office waiting room inscribed with the phrase "United Meritocracy of GitHub."[1] His commitment to meritocracy manifested as a flat organization with no managers, under the assumption that if everyone is competing in a meritocracy, managers are not needed to evaluate performance.[2] GitHub's meritocracy was dominated by men. What did that mean? Logically, if Wanstrath really believed that the best person always wins, the only explanation was that he also believed that women have less merit than men, leading to the inference that women, POC, WOC, and LGBTQ are not as competent.

What many Meritocracy Managers aren't aware of is all of the studies showing that women need to have higher qualifications than men to be given the same opportunities. These studies indicate that women, POC, and WOC are less successful not because they are less accomplished or ambitious but because they are often held to higher standards because of unconscious bias. For example, data show that women are required to have significantly more years of experience than men to be asked to join a corporate board.[3] In my field of academia, female professors have to have stronger publication records to gain tenure and promotion than their male counterparts do.[4]

GitHub ended up becoming a ghost town for women, and many of those who remained described it as a horrible place to work.[5] In 2017, GitHub announced a conference that featured no woman speakers and had to cancel it because of bad press. This is how many Meritocracy Mangers get themselves into trouble. When the lack of diversity in their teams or organization becomes so apparent that others start to speak up, they need to start Inclusifying or they will likely be forced out of their roles.

That was what happened to Wanstrath. When the company was acquired by Microsoft, he was quickly replaced. The new CEO of GitHub, Nat Friedman, says that the company "work[s] hard to build the most inclusive communities we can—online, on our teams, and in cities around the world." Research by Deloitte shows that more inclusive organizations are six times as likely to be innovative, six times as likely to anticipate change and respond effectively, and twice as likely to meet or exceed financial targets. It is notable that over the last year, GitHub experienced an increase from 24 million to 31 million developers and the number of companies using GitHub increased from 1.5 million to 2.1 million.

THE MERITS OF INCLUSIFYING

One of the main obstacles for Meritocracy Managers to becoming Inclusifyers is that they just don't see the benefits of diversity. Because I saw the most Meritocracy Managers in sales, I will make the simple business case for diversity in regard to sales. If you think about it, the United States is becoming more diverse: 43 percent of the 75 million millennials identify as Asian, black, or Hispanic. That is a lot of nonwhite potential customers. The buying power of African Americans is $1.2 trillion and will be $1.5 trillion by 2021. We also know that women make 75 percent of consumer purchasing decisions. If you are going to capture the buying power of women and people of color, you need to understand them. That is why diverse companies are 70 percent more likely to capture new markets than their more homogeneous counterparts are.[6] And this means more sales: a 1 percent increase in gender diversity yields a 3 percent increase in sales, and a 1 percent increase in racial diversity equates to a 9 percent increase in sales.[7]

So if you're sold on becoming an Inclusifyer, I will share a couple of first steps to take toward becoming one: (1) work to enhance fairness by anonymizing assessments and (2) focus on being clearer about how decisions are made by using *aggressive transparency*. Anonymizing assessments increases perceptions of fairness (the F in SELF), which supports uniqueness, whereas being transparent (the T in TEAM) about processes helps people feel that they belong.

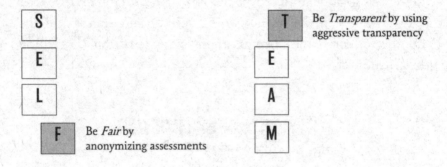

ANONYMIZING ASSESMENTS

Meritocracy Managers often need to see evidence of bias firsthand to get onto the path to Inclusifying. So anonymizing assessments is a great place for Meritocracy Managers to start their Inclusify journey. Jon, an executive at a large financial firm, showed me how effective anonymizing assessments can be in increasing Meritocracy Managers' understanding of bias. He told me that his organization used a variant of anonymizing assessments for their promotions to partner. They wrote two lists of names on the board.

LIST OF PARTNER NOMINEES	LIST OF OBJECTIVELY BEST-PERFORMING EMPLOYEES
John	Ming
David	Jane
Erick	Marco
Peter	Chun

On the left, they wrote the names of all of the nominees for part-ner. On the right, they wrote the names of the top performers based on a variety of different metrics—for example, the individual with the most billable hours, the one with the highest customer satisfaction ratings, the one with the highest subordinate ratings. In this case, Jon said that the list of the best performers contained a large number of Asian Americans, yet no Asians were on the list of part-ner nominees. It made no sense. That's what made him believe that unconscious bias exists, and it made him see the world in a new light.

We see the same thing in STEM professions, where, for example, women have to be 2.5 times as productive as the men in order to be rated as competent.[8] As a result, we see many areas of science in which women are underrepresented; the numbers for ethnic minorities are far worse. The reality is that sometimes people need to see the bias in their organization for themselves for it to become real for them.

I believe in a novel way of mitigating bias—anonymizing assessments—which can be a good first step for Meritocracy Man-agers to take. The idea of anonymizing selection was popularized by the National Symphony Orchestra. As late as the 1970s, the top five orchestras were only 5 percent women. But in the 1970s, or-chestras started using anonymous auditions. Candidates auditioned behind a screen so their gender and race could not be determined. The orchestra went as far as having musicians remove their shoes so no one would hear the *click-clack* of women's high heels.

Even when the anonymous audition was used only for the first round of auditions, it meant that women were 50 percent more likely to move to the finals and became 1.6 times as likely to be selected for the orchestra than when they competed in typical auditions. Today women make up over 30 percent of musicians in the top five orchestras.

I got to see the benefit of this type of intervention firsthand in a project I worked on for the Hubble Space Telescope. The Hubble Space Telescope is a school bus–size orbital telescope that uses a digital camera to take pictures of galaxies, black holes, stars, and planets while it orbits the earth. Because of the enormous value of this tool to researchers, there is a competitive process to secure time on Hubble for research. The process involves submitting a written proposal, which is scored by reviewers. Then the top proposals are discussed in a face-to-face session among the reviewers in which the best proposals are selected.

The process was designed to be meritocratic; the best ideas for the best science would be funded by Hubble, and their generators would be allotted time on the telescope. But the scientists on the Hubble Time Allocation Committee (TAC) noticed that women were less likely to receive time and money than men. The difference was not great, but it had happened every year for more than a decade.

So the committee did something radical. In one of the most profound and effective projects I have ever worked on, it removed applicants' names from the proposals.

The leader who championed this effort was Kenneth Sembach, the director of the Space Telescope Science Institute (STScI) and a professor at Johns Hopkins University. As someone who had worked hard for his position, publishing more than 170 articles in peer-reviewed journals, he believed in meritocracy. But unlike a Meritocracy Manager, he also recognized the potential for a less-than-meritocratic system because of bias. "Certain people have privilege [tailwinds]," he told me at the Hubble Space Telescope offices on Johns Hopkins's Maryland campus. "Maybe it's the school you are at or your past successes, being part of a successful team. All of these things affect how reviewers rate an application. We are not trying to select the people who had the most success in the past; we want to give telescope time to people who have the best ideas for the future, ideas that no one has ever considered or had the technology to test."

When the proposals were anonymized, women outperformed men by almost 1 percent. Though 1 percent may not sound like a lot, with that one change, the bias was broken. We had never suggested that women-led proposals were better than those led by men—just that they were equal. And that shift clearly demonstrated it.

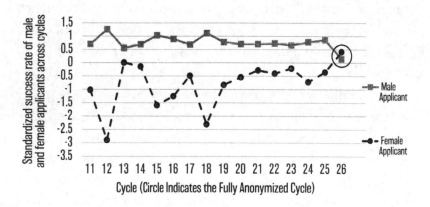

Cycle (Circle Indicates the Fully Anonymized Cycle)

The most powerful part of this strategy is that no one can say that the women received special treatment, because no one knew whose proposal they were reading. The data confirmed the prediction that there had been a subtle bias against women scientists.

At Hubble, I asked folks to think about what they might be

missing out on without the different perspectives that women bring. Ironically, the idea of an orbiting telescope—Hubble—was championed by a woman, Nancy Grace Roman, the first chief astronomer at NASA. Think of what women astrophysicists had discovered thus far, and imagine what more they could have done if they had received equal access to Hubble.

Female astrophysicists have made huge contributions to our body of knowledge. Carolyn Porco found giant geysers of icy particles indicating the presence of water on Saturn's sixth largest moon—a place where previous scientists had not looked. Vera Cooper Rubin introduced us to the idea of invisible dark matter, which was hard to see because it was invisible! Debra Fischer has discovered many planets with their own suns outside our galaxy. Jocelyn Bell Burnell was the first person to hear radio signals coming from space using the first radio telescope, which she created with her PhD adviser. There will always be missed opportunities if we work only with people who look and act and think just like us. What's so great about including different perspectives in a work environment is that it opens up whole new worlds of opportunity.

The data did not only convince me—I'm always aware of the possibility of bias against women. It also convinced people all across the astronomy community—so much so that in 2019, NASA announced that it, too, would adopt the anonymized process.

Anonymizing assessments for selection and promotion:
- Remove names from applications before evaluating them.
- Create a list of the best-qualified candidates versus the nominated candidates for promotion.
- Compare the lists and look for diversity disparities.

When Meritocracy Managers anonymize assessments, their unconscious biases might start to become conscious ones.

USE AGGRESSIVE TRANSPARENCY

With employees' trust in organizations generally low, a lack of transparency can raise suspicions and cause employees to question what their organization is hiding. Women, in particular, believe that a lack of transparency impedes their career progression.[9] Despite the benefits of being transparent, companies seem to be lacking in this regard.[10] In fact, 84 percent of employees say they do not receive enough information from top management. Most say that they look to their immediate supervisor to keep them informed, but this clearly is not working. The fact is, today's employees really want to know about their company, and they say that greater transparency would increase their motivation, help them do their jobs better, and make them less likely to accept a competing offer.[11] In fact, 50 percent of CEOs believe that a lack of trust is a major threat to their organization.[12]

They are right. Not being transparent has real consequences. One study showed that organizations that lack transparency around the recruitment, pay, and promotion of people of color had lower productivity and innovation and higher turnover.[13] Conversely, increasing transparency not only has positive impacts on performance but can also be effective in increasing diversity and inclusion.[14] It's one of the easiest ways to increase trust.[15]

Increasing transparency will require you to consider *how* you are setting the criteria for "best person for the job." Try to research all of the nuances of *how* promotions are made, *how* pay is determined, *how* anyone gets into the high-potential pool. Then examine those practices to see if there's any way they could be biased. Is there an alternative avenue that could make the workplace more equitable? Share the results with your employees. Let them know *how* promotion decisions are made, *what* key experiences they need to have, and *when* they should be trying to get them. By being transparent, you can also increase performance and increase employees' sense of belonging by focusing on the *team*. Indeed, increasing transparency can cause individuals to feel more like organizational insiders, which increases their engagement and ownership of their jobs.[16]

Being more transparent can impact bottom-line outcomes. Knowing how decisions are made can improve performance, particularly when married to increased diversity. A study by Cloverpop, a software company that uses artificial intelligence to make decisions, examined 566 business decisions made by 184 different business teams in a wide variety of companies over two years. They found that diverse teams usually make better decisions than homogenous teams. However, it was not just diversity that mattered; transparency also played a role. Teams that were diverse but lacked decision-making transparency benefited less from their diversity.

This suggests that information should be pushed out to employees on a regular basis.[17] You should tell people:

- When you are making a decision
- What you decide
- Who are the people involved
- Who is affected

The researchers also suggest sharing company benchmarks, processes, and practices and, even more important, getting input on those decisions.

But transparency cannot just be sending company emails or providing access to look up information. Passive transparency is sharing the information for those who want to look. Aggressive transparency is *making* them look. This means that if you want to be transparent with your salary data, you don't just make it available, you create infographics, you tweet about it, you post on Instagram or on the company's intranet or put signs around the office.

Importantly, transparency cannot just come out of nowhere. In *The Speed of Trust: The One Thing That Changes Everything*, Stephen M. R. Covey said that transparency is one of the fastest ways to build trust and feelings of belonging but noted that it takes a good communication strategy in order to do it well.[18] A sudden slap of transparency can upset the system if it is not balanced by other information. For example, just posting everyone's salary information without also conducting a salary audit or having a plan for repairing salary discrepancies can create havoc among employees.

The question is, if you are not being transparent with information, what are you hiding? And if your practices are broken, hiding the information is not going to help. Being honest and making progress on fixing things for the better is the Inclusifyer way to go. Transparency helps people feel as though they are on the inside and part of the team.

With the goal of providing more transparency, more and more companies are sharing their data on gender and racial diversity on their websites. Being transparent about outcomes is good. But what about also being transparent about practices? If everyone knew how promotions were made or how salary was determined, it might solve the problem that in today's world it can seem as though everyone—men, women, majority, minority—feels discriminated against. If everyone thinks the system is against them, maybe we need to be clearer about how the system works.

Chapter 6

CULTURE CRUSADER

The Curse of Crusading While Homogeneous

*It's a chemistry argument, and I don't think you would ever hire
somebody whose chemistry doesn't fit the culture that you want.*
—SENIOR LEADER, FINANCE

CULTURE CRUSADER: ORIGINS

Organizational culture is the shared understanding of the beliefs,
expectations, values, and norms that are exemplified through
employees' collective patterns of language and behavior; it is re-
inforced by the organization's systems and practices. Anyone who
has ever been a part of a great team knows the magic that having
a strong shared culture can bring. I see it on the most effective
corporate boards, in the most successful top management teams,
in the greatest bands, in the best sports teams. When people feel

as though they're really connected, work feels more like play and their coworkers become their closest friends.

It comes as no surprise, then, that you want to replicate this feeling and create a team where everyone understands each other, everyone gets along, and you all share the same values. If you have a strong desire to achieve esprit de corps, tend to hire people who are culturally similar to you, and encourage fitting in over standing out, you could be a Culture Crusader.

You might look at your team and celebrate your culture but notice that those who don't fit into that culture tend to feel excluded. Or you might worry that you're missing perspectives or opportunities by stacking a team with people who are quite similar to one another. It is possible that you have explained this away by telling yourself that "they" don't fit the culture or "they" don't want to work there. Lots of Culture Crusaders feel this way. But those who look inward at potential flaws in their own system instead of outward at flaws in others' are likely to excel at Inclusifying. As a Culture Crusader, you are already adept at creating the feeling of belonging; now you just need to create uniqueness.

Birds of a Feather

Wanting to be around similar people is not a crime. We all experience more chemistry with those who are similar to us than with those who aren't. It's just like dating: people like to say that opposites attract, but the data don't support that idea. Instead, "birds of a feather flock together," and we are more likely to marry someone who shares our religion, profession, race, socioeconomic background, and even looks than we are to marry someone who is different from us. This is the basic underpinning of in-group bias—the idea that we favor people who are in our group and avoid people who are not.

It should come as no surprise, then, that when companies are interested in creating good chemistry or culture, leaders look to hire people who are just like themselves. The tendency to gravitate toward people who are the most similar to us is called homophile, or similar-to-me, bias. I have seen this to be especially true on corporate boards. I interviewed CEOs and chairs from gender-diverse boards in S&P Composite 1500 firms to learn about why there is not more diversity on corporate boards. One chair told me that boards lack diversity because of fear of the unknown and that it might upset the great culture that the board has created. "If you make me trade between somebody I know and I'm comfortable with and somebody I don't know who's a woman or minority, I'll take somebody I'm comfortable with. I'm not discriminating. I'm just telling you that I would pick somebody that I know and I'm familiar with before I would pick somebody I didn't know.

"It feels like a Thanksgiving dinner kind of thing," he continued. "I'm going to see these folks every so often and it's going to be in a confined space and we're going to have to deal with some hard subjects, so I want to *like* who is seated to the left and the right of me. It's about chemistry."

If this feels true to you—if you believe culture fit is the most important thing, if you find yourself around a lot of people who are quite similar to you, if you think it is just easier to hire people you already know—you may have elements of a Culture Crusader in you. But here is the problem: even though we think that working with people we know will facilitate group decision-making, the data suggest otherwise.

Diverse Flocks Make Better Decisions

In a study of GitHub programmers, scientists compared the performance of teams with two members who had worked together previously to those with members who had not. The diverse duos—who had not previously worked together—performed nearly *eight times* as well as those who had more experience working together.[1] Working with new people translates to better performance.

There is also something that changes about group processes when groups are more diverse. For example, one research study on decision-making found that the members of racially diverse groups share more information with one another, which leads to better performance.[2] In the study, researchers created groups of three students who were either all white or two white and one nonwhite. The team members were supposed to play a murder mystery game, with each team member receiving some clues that only he or she had. To solve the mystery, the team members needed to share their unique information. The interesting result was that the members of diverse teams were more likely to share the information that only they had and performed better.

THE FOLLY OF THE CULTURE CRUSADER

In many ways, the idea of culture fit was popularized by the founders of PayPal (sometimes called the PayPal mafia), who espoused the idea that for a company to be successful, its employees have to be similar to one another. They promoted the idea that new hires should be people you would "want to have a beer with." Max Levchin, one of the founders of PayPal, says that the company actually disqualified an applicant because he liked to play basketball, which suggested that he would not fit in with the nerdy culture at PayPal. Levchin was quoted in *Forbes* back in 2007 as saying, "All of this is about self-selecting for people just like you. He thinks like me, he's just as geeky, and he doesn't get laid very often. Great hire! We'll get along perfectly." But he also admitted that PayPal's culture of "nerdiness and alpha-maleness" was problematic in that it created a difficult fit for women.[3] That meant that women might have been less likely to take a job at PayPal and might have been more likely to quit if they felt that they did not fit in.

Groupthink

Culture Crusaders cultivate a cohesive but limited culture that creates empty spaces where a fresh or unique perspective could point out problems, highlight opportunities, or predict disruption. The fact is that when teams are highly similar and highly cohesive, they are at greater risk of conformity and groupthink. Conformity can cause teams to make poor decisions, such as those outlined in research on groupthink. The social psychologist Solomon Asch demonstrated the problem of groupthink in a classic study on conformity. An experimenter drew four lines on the board like those below. He asked three students (plants who are in on the study) which line was the most similar to line X. They all said A (even though the answer is B). When the experimenter called on the fourth person, the only real participant, he also said A. This is how groupthink or conformity works; people would rather knowingly make a mistake than buck the group consensus.

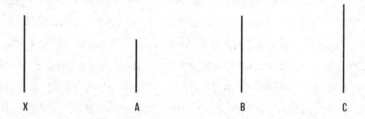

Now, how does groupthink relate to diversity? Researchers recently redid this experiment but chose confederates (those who were in on the experiment) of different races. What did they find? Participants did not conform to the group's opinion when the group contained members of a different race than themselves. When the confederates were homogeneous, 32 percent of people conformed compared to 20 percent when they were diverse.[4] It would seem that we are less willing to conform to people who are different from us, which is great to know! If conformity results in poor decision-making over time and a lack of diversity makes conformity more likely to occur, diversity is the answer to improving your rate of good decision-making.

Lord of the Flies

There is another problem associated with Culture Crusading. Maybe it is because many Culture Crusader companies grew out of Silicon Valley or maybe it is just coincidence, but many of the Culture Crusaders I met were smart and highly competitive people, and also aggressive. Their belief in blunt feedback translated to lots of yelling to make sure their ideas were heard. For example, PayPal's culture was highly critical, and employees routinely raised their voices and tore one another down. Disputes between employees were routinely resolved by wrestling matches in the office. Wrestling matches!

But years of psychology research on aggression have shown us how fear and bullying escalate over time to create a toxic culture. In addition to the fact that an aggressive atmosphere excludes people who "can't take it," there is strong and consistent evidence that even among those who say they like ferocious competition, experience greater levels of depression, anxiety, and intentions to quit. In fact, men who "can take it" actually suffer from higher levels of depression, anxiety, alcohol abuse, and even suicide than do others. And because it would violate their gender norm of toughness, they rarely seek support to help them cope.[5] Basically, those who can't take it leave, and those who can take it just suffer.

The results are so negative that workers and companies are starting to crack down on bullying at work. For example, women at Nike sued the organization for failing to control a culture of bullying and harassment that they claim diminished women's career success. The lawsuit resulted in eleven executives being ousted in 2018 and an additional lawsuit by shareholders who claim that their shares lost value because the board and leadership team failed to act on the toxic culture that affected women, POC, WOC, and LGBTQ.[6] Likewise, in July 2018, a Credit Suisse banker, Paul Dexter, made headlines when he was fired over a complaint of inappropriately bullying a *male* intern because the behavior violated the organization's no-harassment policy.[7]

THE MAIN MISTAKE AND MYTH AT THE HEART OF CULTURE CRUSADING

The Mistake of Letting Fun Become Dysfunctional

One of the simplest mistakes a Culture Crusader can make is letting the pursuit of fun become dysfunctional. Cultures can become invisible to those who are in them, according to Jordan Belfort, the real person behind Leonardo DiCaprio's character in the 2013 movie *The Wolf of Wall Street*. Belfort was described as creating a drug-fueled macho culture in an investment firm—and he eventually went to jail for securities fraud.[8] Belfort and I both spoke at the Harvard Negotiation & Leadership Conference in 2016. I talked about bias, and he talked about ethics.

Belfort's story was very similar to those of many Culture Crusaders I spoke with. He was trying to make the workplace a fun environment and create a place where everyone could connect and belong. In Belfort's case, he modeled his behavior after Gordon Gekko, from the 1987 movie *Wall Street*. He says that he was only behaving in the way he had been taught, mimicking the behavior he had learned on the playground and seen in movies. The result was a culture that spiraled out of control and left him and the rest of the team in shambles.

In fact, there's an evolutionary reason behind this kind of behavior. Our brains are rigged to scrutinize negative situations to protect us from danger. So if someone tries to convince you to engage in risky behavior when you're in a bad mood, you are not likely to be persuaded. In contrast, when we think about having fun, it activates the part of our brain that causes us to go for it without thinking too much about the consequences. So if someone tries to convince you to do something risky when you're experiencing positive emotions such as anticipatory enthusiasm, amusement, or romantic love, you can be more easily convinced.[9]

If this sounds like an outdated 1980s sort of thing, remember that it was only in 2018 that the sports apparel company Under Armour passed a rule that employees could no longer fund trips to strip clubs on the company's dime![10] It should be no surprise to learn that companies that allow sexually charged office parties fueled by drugs and alcohol, such as those documented by Emily Chang in the book *Brotopia: Breaking Up the Boys' Club of Silicon Valley*, can also have a dysfunctional culture.[11] As she discovered, women who attended the sex parties were judged negatively, while those who did not missed out on important business opportunities. Chang also noted that there was no room for gay men or religious people in this type of scene.

Working in an environment in which women are sexualized diminishes female employees' feelings of self-worth. When the behavior is directed at them, it can negatively impact their perfor-mance. For example, one research study showed that when women experienced a sexualized gaze from confederates (people who were in on the study), it caused them to perform more poorly on a series of math problems and GRE test items.[12]

The problem, as Chang noted, is that business is done at toxic events—which creates disparities in access to resources. Indeed, peo-ple who drink tend to earn 10 to 14 percent more money than their sober counterparts, highlighting the inequity that can arise when certain people are excluded from socializing because they don't imbibe.[13]

It is possible to be proactive and think about how all of your cultural activities might be perceived by women, the LGBTQ community, and certain religious communities. Those that might alienate parts of the organization can be swapped out for new ac-tivities that will be more inclusive to everyone.

INCLUSIFYING ACTION: Culture Swap

OLD CULTURAL ACTIVITY	NEW INCLUSIFYED CULTURAL ACTIVITY
Drinking heavily at a bar	Having appetizers and light drinks at a restaurant
Going to strip clubs	Holding potluck lunches
Hunting on the weekend	Volunteering in the community
Holding a sexy Halloween party	Celebrating lots of different cultural events
Holding male-only golf outings	Holding birthday social events each month
Encouraging men's poker and cigars	Holding a coed poker challenge
Paintballing	Going to an escape room together
Playing basketball	Watching a basketball game together

The Myth That Words Don't Matter

Another drawback of a culturally homogeneous workplace is that your language can become outdated. It might be common to refer to certain things as "retarded," refer to women as "hon," or even joke around about "getting laid." Offensive or crass language marks your team as backward and outdated, but it is easy to let a culture obscure the importance of using language that does not negatively impact others.

One of my former students told me that the language of his company culture on Wall Street was so toxic it had made him quit his job. After leaving the socially liberal environment of CU Boulder, Marty was surprised to hear antigay slurs in his office on a daily basis. "That's so gay," people would say in response to things they did not like. At a bar, when he would call it a night before his co-workers did, he was called a "fag" or "pussy."

"It made me so uncomfortable to be around this all the time," he said. "I finally asked my friend John, 'Can you use a word other than "fag"? What if one of our coworkers is gay?'" His concern for others prompted Marty's coworkers to start calling him a homo. Someone would call a woman who had rejected him a dyke, and then another coworker would say, "Watch it—Marty's a homo." "If I were gay, I would probably have gone to HR, but as a straight man, I was not sure how I could complain that I just don't like assholes." It was not long before Marty started looking for a job elsewhere.

INCLUSIFYING ACTION: **You wouldn't program in MS-DOS; learn the language.**

Although these elements of language can become ingrained in our culture, many organizations have formal policies against hate speech and using it is enough to get a CEO or any leader tossed out of the company. But when leaders find themselves in a cultural echo chamber, they can lose touch with what constitutes professional communication. That's how you get someone making statements like "We call that Boob-er." That was what the founder of Uber, Travis Kalanick, said in response to the question about his success with women.[14] Not long after, Uber was hit with a gender discrimination and sexual harassment lawsuit by women such as Susan Fowler, a former Uber employee who publicly wrote about sexual harassment at the company.[15] Like many Culture Crusaders who fall, Kalanick was ousted by his board and executive team and even sued for a breach of his fiduciary duties to the organization.[16]

Maybe you feel frustrated. It feels impossible to keep up with the constantly shifting politically correct terminology. For example, you might call a woman from Barbados African American, even though she identifies as black. Are people from Mexico Latino, Hispanic, or Mexican? (Yes to all.) People indigenous to the United States might prefer being called Native American rather than Indian. People from India might identify as South Asian, and people from Japan or Singapore are not Chinese.

You think that the cultural differences between Mexico and Puerto Rico are negligible or that because their inhabitants are all Latino, the specifics don't matter. But when you don't take the time to learn the language, you're communicating to your team members that the specifics of their identity aren't important to you—that *they're* not important to you. Is that the impression you want to make?

Language 101

You can learn a little about the terms by doing some research. But more important, leaders need to be open to hearing the message that their language is off. When my friend from Puerto Rico was called Mexican by her Culture Crusader boss, she said, "I'm actually Puerto Rican."

What not to say:
"It doesn't really matter, you're all Latino."
"I can't keep up with all this PC bullshit."
"Don't call HR on me."

What an Inclusifyer would say:
"I did not know that; thank you for telling me."
"Sorry—my mistake."
"I don't know much about Puerto Rico. If you have time, I would
    love to learn more."

Inclusifyers know that their words matter, and they work to learn to communicate more effectively. If you start with a sense of curiosity about your team, you'll learn so much more than just the right words to use; you'll learn how to show your team members that they matter.

It seems pretty obvious that there is no room for hate language in Inclusifyed businesses, but there are more subtle ways that language can hurt. Hateful terms such as "bitch" and "battle-ax" are used to disparage women, but even language that sounds endearing can undermine them. Calling women "sweet," "playful," "darling," or anything that sounds as though you're talking about a kid is outdated.

No Girls Allowed

One quick way to sound more Inclusifyed is to stop calling women "girls." An accountant named Todd told me, "I've heard some of our senior partners . . . they'll be talking with a client and say, 'She's a great girl,' in reference to one of our young female staff. She just went from twenty-three to five. And it's already hard for a twenty-three-year-old to establish themselves in front of an executive. They didn't mean anything by it, but every word matters." But when Todd told a senior partner that he shouldn't call the female staff "girls," the exec blew Todd off, saying that he's old and to him they are girls. They are as young as his daughter.

I laughed when I heard that anecdote, although it really explains a lot: that manager would rather disrespect his coworker than consider changing his choice of words. Just a few weeks later, I was visiting a colleague's class, and he actually introduced me to the class as a "great girl." My postdoc stared at me to see what I would say. "You know, at forty years old, no one has called me a girl for twenty years. And even then I was kinda surprised by it." No one laughed. My postdoc later joked that I should start a blog called *Girlprof* (like *Girlboss*). It is not that being called a girl is inherently offensive, it's that his words undercut some of my authority to the students in the class. Would he have said, "He's a great boy," had I been male? Of course not, because that would have made me sound juvenile. Yet women are diminished to "girls" in the workplace every day.

Inclusifyers take it upon themselves to update their cultural communication skills. They stay up to date with the business world. Updating your skills is a common workplace practice. If you used to code with C++, you don't just keep using it because that is what you are used to, right? You have to keep up with coding language and learn Python and SQL. And if you're falling behind, it means it's time to learn a new language. Doing so will help you connect with and create stronger connections with all of the members of your team—which will make you a better leader.

Chapter 7

LEADERSHIP STRATEGIES FOR CULTURE CRUSADERS

We have a very diverse board of directors at Alaska (50 percent of independent directors are women) and we have seen firsthand how the discussions and the decisions improve when people around the table are more diverse.

—BRAD TILDEN, CEO, ALASKA AIR GROUP (INCLUSIFYER)

Brian Chesky, the CEO of Airbnb, was truly great at building belonging as part of the culture of his online property rental marketplace. He cared about culture so much that it drove him to sit in on the interviews of the first three hundred employees at the now $30 billion company. He knew that the first people he hired would be the model for all of the future employees in the organization, and he wanted to choose a group of people who believed in the mission and values of Airbnb.

So he did. He created a spectacularly cohesive team of similar individuals. Cohesive culture, as we have learned, has a downside. When everyone thinks the same way, they are more vulnerable to groupthink and poor decision-making.

And that was what happened. When a 2014 Harvard study revealed discrimination at Airbnb, the company of similar individuals did not know what to do and failed to take action. In the study, researchers created twenty identical user profiles, except that the names were changed to be either black or white sounding. They sent 6,400 messages to Airbnb owners expressing interest in renting the properties. They found that about 50 percent of "white" inquiries were accepted, but only 42 percent of "black" inquiries were accepted. That 8 percent difference is felt by Airbnb users of color, who always have to question whether a "booked" property would have been available to a white renter.[1]

For example, one Airbnb customer, Gregory Selden, applied to rent a property as himself (a black man, using a photo of himself) and as a white man (using a photo of someone else), finding that the same property owner claimed that the space was booked when he applied as himself but was available for his white alter ego.[2] A year later, a different property owner canceled a reservation by Dyne Suh via text messages that read, "One word says it all. Asian." And "I wouldn't rent it to u if u were the last person on earth."[3]

But Chesky realized that the company's shortcomings were due to a lack of diversity, and he committed to creating a more heterogeneous organization because he believed that it would create a better product.

Airbnb has made great strides in increasing its diversity and building a more inclusive culture.[4] Chesky set targets for increasing diversity among the company's employees by the end of 2017. He committed to diversity in race and gender on the finalist slates of all senior-level positions. And he changed the company's culture and values to include *diversity* while maintaining his commitment to *belonging*. He made the commitment to Inclusify. For example, the company now hosts surprise birthday parties and baby showers and celebrates other important events in people's lives. This helps increase the team bonding needed to develop a sense of belonging.

Inclusifying gives Culture Crusaders the opportunity to capitalize on their stellar culture-building skills, but in a new way that creates committed cultures of inclusion while optimizing employees' feelings of uniqueness. In this chapter, I provide three strategies for Inclusifying: inclusifying your cultural values and behaviors, going for rogues, and crafting culture crews. All you need to do is use your skills for motivating others through all aspects of the organization, including its culture, and pivot so that those values are Inclusifyed. You can also increase learning and create new perspectives by hiring people who are not the norm, which I call *Going for Rogues*, and you can empower your team by crafting culture crews.

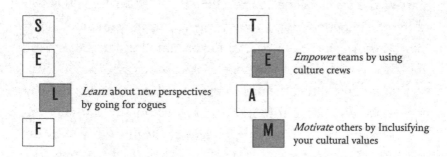

S

E

L   *Learn* about new perspectives by going for rogues

F

T

E   *Empower* teams by using culture crews

A

M   *Motivate* others by Inclusifying your cultural values

INCLUSIFY YOUR CULTURAL VALUES AND BEHAVIORS (MOTIVATE)

Inclusifying your cultural values is important for any leader but plays to Culture Crusaders' strength as culture builders. Updating culture is just like so many other aspects of business: difficult but necessary if you don't want to become obsolete. But how is a leader supposed to see that culture change is needed, much less start making changes? That is the question I posed to the CEO of the company that started the Culture Crusader movement, PayPal.

Starting in 2014, when PayPal hired a new CEO, Dan Schulman, I noticed many articles about the positive changes being implemented at the company. I had been impressed with PayPal's positions on banning hate groups from using its platform and taking a stand against anti-LGBTQ legislation. But I have to admit, I was still surprised when Schulman agreed to talk with me. Knowing PayPal's history—remember, this is the company that started out by hiring people with whom managers would "want to have a beer"—I wasn't sure what he would say when I asked him for his thoughts about Inclusifying.

But Schulman proved to me that an Inclusifyer can change an organization's culture if he or she makes diversity and inclusion part of the fabric of the business. He said, "Diversity is the right thing to do, period. But if you can tie it into your mission and vision, it brings both your heart and your intellectual sides coming together. I think when that happens, it's extraordinarily powerful."

Schulman said that the mission of PayPal is to democratize payments, so it was crucial to him to have a similarly equitable and inclusive culture. He had some work to do, beginning with assessing the culture, conveying Inclusifyed values, and then ensuring that structures and practices were applied in a way that supported the company's core values.

In an open letter to PayPal employees he said that his goal is to "create an environment where our colleagues, customers and partners see PayPal as a place where they can experience a sense of uniqueness and a sense of belonging." He was using the Inclusify playbook.

Schulman also took action to create diversity. When PayPal found a pay gap between men and women in 2015, Schulman faced a bit of resistance over the millions of dollars it would cost to fix it. But the company made the commitment, conducted the pay gap analysis, and adjusted the pay of all of its twenty thousand employees. Ensuring that people are paid fairly is an example of how to match your structures with your values. Without that alignment, employees will lose trust in the authenticity of those values.

Despite the logic that paying people more could hurt its bottom line, in 2018, PayPal became one of the highest-valued US companies with over 300 million active accounts (consumers and merchants) as of November 2019. In the third quarter of 2019, for the first time ever, PayPal processed more than 1 billion transactions per month in a single quarter and had a market cap of approximately $120 billion. PayPal was named in the top ten of Just Capital and *Forbes*'s Just 100 list for 2019, featuring "companies doing right by America." PayPal was named number eight overall (out of 922 companies considered) and number one in the commercial support and services industry (out of 38 companies on the list). PayPal's CEO attributes at least some of the company's innovation and growth to the Inclusifyed culture it has adopted, which began with a focus on increasing diversity.

Innovation Is the Answer

Schulman is not wrong. Numerous statistics link diversity to innovation. One study revealed that greater gender diversity in top management among S&P Composite 1500 firms yielded greater financial returns, and that effect was found particularly among companies that valued innovation.[5] In a review of national banks, another study found the same thing for race: racial diversity was positively related to financial performance, and that was particularly true of banks that valued innovation.[6] A third study showed that companies with more diversity programs—from disability to gender to race to LGBTQ status—created two more products a year than did companies that did not have diversity programs.[7] *Two more products!* So if you want to encourage innovation, diversity can be a great place to start. The questions for Culture Crusaders are, how can you increase diversity and then what can you do to yield its innovation benefits?

GO FOR ROGUES (LEARN)

Culture Crusaders are master team builders, but their teams and organizations often lack different perspectives because their members are hired for sameness (culture fit) rather than diversity. Many Culture Crusaders I spoke with also suggested that "'they' [diverse talent] don't want to work here" because "they" don't fit in. I remember watching the talk show host David Letterman interview the comedian Tina Fey some time ago. She asked him why he had not hired more woman writers for his show. "I don't know—maybe they did not want the job?" he responded. And why were there no people of color on the team? It might be true that they would find the culture tough to fit into, but who would not want to write for a top show? "No, they wanted the job," Fey wryly replied.

At the most basic level, this means that Culture Crusaders need to let go of the idea that "they don't want to work here," stop hiring for sameness (culture fit), and become more intentional about bringing in the necessary differences of thought (and variety of hires) to ensure that there are different viewpoints to share. This will allow everyone to learn from those differences. Further, by bringing in new perspectives, Inclusifyers show people that they value uniqueness and want to learn from people holding different views.

How can one encourage diversity and variety of thought and perspective? One way is to hire and promote people who don't fit your culture but do add to it, so that you can learn from their perspectives. The kind of people I call rogues will help generate new discussions and improve innovation and decision-making.

This means examining your team and considering what perspectives you could be missing out on. This is what a finance executive, Mindy, told me about her decision to go for rogues. Although there were a lot of women at her firm, she realized they were still very homogenous. So when a white guy with a Mohawk and tie-dyed shirt came into her office for an interview, she thought, maybe he is the person we need to help us understand our customers and business in a new way. Rather than writing him off or pretending he did not have a Mohawk, she slowed down for a minute and asked him what he could bring to the table. And because he turned out to be able to reach a new market of millennials and Gen Zers, Mindy told me that going for that rogue really paid off.

It is still so easy to choose people we know and like and who are similar to us. This is why so many of the board chairs I interviewed explained that board members just prefer to sit with people they know. It does facilitate making quick, unquestioned decisions—but at the cost of the best, most innovative, most complete solutions.

Not a Problem

To show this effect, researchers recruited three-person teams from the same sorority or fraternity to identify a fictitious murderer based on fake detectives' interviews.[8] We all know that sororities and fraternities breed cohesion. But, in this case, five minutes into the discussion they were joined by a fourth person—sometimes from the same fraternity or sorority, sometimes not. On the homogeneous teams everyone understood one another, conversation was fluid, and the students all got along well. But their ease of interaction came at a cost to their performance. Having someone "different" join their group caused the students to feel as though they were less effective and actually made them feel as though they made worse decisions—but they were wrong. Adding an outsider as opposed to an insider actually doubled their chance of identifying the murderer, from 29 percent to 60 percent. Their decision-making felt more difficult, but their outcome was better. Diverse teams make better decisions than homogeneous, cohesive teams do.

Many Inclusifying leaders share the same philosophy. Dan Schulman explained that when he joined PayPal, as at lots of software companies, his board was 90 percent white men—and the one woman on the board was someone he brought in with him. Two years later, the board has five white men, three women, one African American man, and one Hispanic man. I was impressed. But my esteem for Schulman only grew as he articulated how the diversity on his board has really served to add to the company culture. "It's not just a symbol," he said. "Diversity creates different points of view and perspectives, different ways of approaching topics, different ways of analyzing topics. Just different thought patterns.".

Although diversity can take many different forms, all of the benefits of diversity can be achieved by hiring people from different social categories than your own, whether race, gender, or sexual orientation.[9] And there is one more reason to hire people who are in a different social category from yours: it will actually make you better. When you believe that you are going to have to convince a diverse group of people, you actually work harder and prepare a more thoughtful argument than when you believe that you have to convince only people who are similar to you.[10]

The lesson is: go for rogues, and then learn from them.

CRAFT CULTURE CREWS (EMPOWER)

Culture Crusaders need to communicate to their teams that they value different perspectives. One way to do that is to craft culture crews—groups of diverse people from across the organization—who are empowered to make decisions. Culture crews break down silos by operating like cross-functional task forces. Anyone can create culture crews by determining an organizational opportunity for change, assembling a group of people from different departments, divisions, or levels, and having them work together to solve the problem. You can do this with one crew or assemble a few crews and let them tackle the same or different problems.

The Medici Group

Frans Johansson, CEO of the Medici Group (Medici) and the author of *The Medici Effect: Breakthrough Insights at the Intersection of Ideas, Concepts, and Cultures* and *The Click Moment: Seizing Opportunity in an Unpredictable World*, has built an entire organization around the definitive strategy for using diversity and inclusion as a driver of innovation. For more than a decade, Johansson and Medici have helped hundreds of executive leaders and thousands of teams to increase effectiveness and collaboration across silos, increase speed, and launch bold new products and services.

As I sat in his office on the twenty-sixth floor of the Regus

Business Center on Third Avenue in Manhattan, Johansson told me about one of his newest clients, ESPN. At the time, Medici and Johansson had a plan to drive innovation at ESPN by connecting diversity and inclusion to their global growth goals, expanding top leaders' mind-sets, and leveraging their existing geographical diversity. Now, almost two years later, ESPN reports that its digital and print unit grew its global fan base by 60 percent, resulting in 120 million monthly visitors to its sites.

Why does building diverse and inclusive teams work? In large organizations, there are many people with different sets of knowledge stemming from their gender, race, country of origin, education, functional background, and personality. Unfortunately, these people rarely share their information because everyone is focused on getting his or her own job done. When you desire innovation, however, you can widen your creative pool by bringing teams together to share their perspectives. Due to shared information bias, we usually spend more time and energy discussing shared rather than unshared information; it is simply less difficult to discuss things that everyone already knows. But when you bring together a diverse and inclusive group, its members are less likely to assume that everyone else has the same background knowledge, so they start to reframe opportunities and challenges, unlock new pathways, move faster, reallocate resources, and collaborate more effectively.

Medtronic

I thought it was a great idea at the time and I have never heard anything like it until I found myself at the Boulder office of global medical device company Medtronic. I was there giving a talk about diversity and inclusion when one of its employees mentioned that she had learned a lot about inclusion by participating in cross-functional task forces at Medtronic. What she described sounded much like what Johansson does as a consultant, but internally for an entire organization.

When Medtronic acquired Covidien, it was the largest deal in medical device history. One of the best practices that was quickly leveraged across the company during integration was a program known as "Culture Circles." These small cross-functional task forces helped to address any culture clash caused by the merger, building change agility as an organizational competency. In addition to the meaningful development (employees who participate in culture circles are three times more likely to get promoted than those who don't participate) and retention (employees who participate in culture circles are seven times more likely to stay at Medtronic than those who don't participate) drivers, employees describe this as an empowerment movement that naturally drives inclusion. Medtronic's CEO was quoted during the 2017 Wallin Leadership Awards, saying, "Culture Circles are arguably as the most influential inclusion effort within MITG" (Minimally Invasive Therapies Group [MITG] is comprised mostly of the Covidien business that Medtronic acquired).

This inclusion becomes most evident toward the end of the program, after individuals from cross-functional areas around the world work to solve an organizational challenge that shows up locally, in their subculture. Culture Circles has a capstone training called "Leadership Labs," where they have a huge competition and celebration for the best ideas. I sat in on one of those labs and saw how the competition actually created collaboration and cohesion. At the end, the winner is announced in an auditorium filled with hundreds of screaming fans—the members of the Culture Circles.

As a guest at the 2017 Culture Circle event in Denver, I was a bit overwhelmed as I walked to the front of the crowded ball-room to give my remarks. People in the room were cheering and laughing. I felt as if I were in the middle of pro soccer game. I said something—and I honestly cannot remember what. But everyone cheered, and I had my own personal rock-star moment. More important, I experienced the sense of confidence and camaraderie that Inclusifyed culture bestows on its members.

There are many different ways to form teams like this; for example, you could post the opportunity to solve an organizational issue (like a task force aimed at measuring inclusion in the organization) and assemble the most diverse teams that you can based on who volunteers. You could also handpick people from across the organization and invite them to serve on the team. Regardless of how the team comes together, the fundamental goal is to empower people from diverse backgrounds and parts of the organization to solve an organizational problem.

MD Anderson Cancer Center

Two years after the Medtronic bash, I was at a board meeting (I serve on an advisory board at MD Anderson Cancer Center) and I heard culture crews mentioned again by R. Kevin Grigsby, the senior director of leadership and talent development at the Association of American Medical Colleges. He said that he uses culture crews all of the time to enhance culture and unite employees of diverse health disciplines, functional areas, ethnicities, socioeconomic classes, genders, and sexual orientations. In fact, he had used them when he had served as a dean at the University of Pennsylvania when he wanted to find ways to address perceived inequities across the medical campus.

In his intervention, medical personnel formed eight cross-departmental teams to find solutions to the greatest challenges faced at the university related to its mission, resources, and relationships.[11] The interdisciplinary teams worked together and came up with solutions that addressed all of the unique perspectives held across the campus. Based on survey data Grigsby collected over multiple years, the teams improved processes, productivity, and people's perceptions of the on-campus culture.

Although diversity is inherent in the design of culture crews, none of the examples I shared made people feel as though they were participating in diversity training. Instead, by bringing together their unique perspectives and empowering teams to act, they drove diversity and inclusion goals.

Chapter 8

TEAM PLAYER

Taking the "Me" Out of "Team"

I've been part of hen parties, and it was absolutely awful. I was one of five women who worked for a woman. I couldn't stand it because she constantly wanted us to do things together like go shopping. I'm not kidding. I was like "What the hell?"
—*FEMALE EXECUTIVE, RETAIL*

TEAM PLAYER: ORIGINS

Team Players are a subset of Culture Crusaders. If you are a woman (or possibly a minority or LGBTQ person) and the Culture Crusader chapter resonated with you because you believe in the importance of creating an effective workplace through culture but the leadership style was not quite you, you could be a Team Player. Just about any woman who says "my worst boss was a woman" has a little Team Player in her.

Many women, POC, WOC, and LGBTQ I have spoken with have described their own career path as difficult. And if you climbed the corporate ladder in the 1970s, '80s, or '90s, that was probably true for you. No one "lowered the bar" for you or gave you "special treatment" along the way. You definitely did not have the help of many women above you; there probably were few to be found, or you may have felt as though your worst bosses were other women.

But as a result, your own success is sweeter. It proves that you had what it took to persevere. And you continue to hold other women, POC, WOC, and LGBTQ to the same standard. You feel as though you support other women (or minorities), of course, but you expect them to work as hard to succeed as you did.

Maybe you feel that you are not a typical woman in that you have chosen to invest in your career over family or you don't identify with most of the other women in your office. Or if you are a POC, do you think you are not typical for your minority group in a myriad of ways? That, too, is a sign you are a Team Player.

DANCING IN THE DISTANCE

In almost all cases, Team Players have two things in common. First, they persevered despite a tough road in their own careers, and second, they don't identify much with their own group, say, a typical black man, a typical woman, a typical gay or disabled person. Instead, they tend to identify with the majority group—white men.

Considering the rough treatment many endure, it's not surprising that lots of women and some minorities want to fit in rather than emphasize their gender or racial group. But whatever the reason, not everyone sees his or her race or gender as part of his or her central identity. The Christian evangelical author, actress, and speaker Priscilla Shirer, who is African American, stated in a video on Facebook that she does not identify as a black woman, only as a Christian. She said, "I don't want 'black,' my race, to be my defining adjective as a woman. . . . I am not a black woman, I'm a Christian woman who happens to be black." Her identity is as a Christian and as a woman, but she does not identify with her race. Her critics accuse her of trying to fit in with right-wing Christians by distancing herself from her identity as a black woman.

I see Team Player behaviors most commonly among women, but there is also evidence that some gay men adopt hypermasculine traits to distance themselves from effeminate stereotypes. POC sometimes do something similar. The social distancing strategy allows people to avoid or escape the social disadvantages of their group.[1]

We All Want to Be on the Best Team

On some level, we all want to be associated with the winning team. I am not a huge sports fan, but as a Denver resident, when the Broncos made it to the Super Bowl, I wanted to buy an orange T-shirt. I wanted to have that sense of group identity and be part of a winning team (of fans). I had the same feeling when the Colorado Rockies went to the World Series back in 2007.

But there are some people who identify with their team so strongly that they'd fight you if you questioned their loyalty. They are there when the team is doing well, and they are there when they are 2–10. I think of so many Green Bay Packers fans I knew when I lived in Wisconsin. For those fans, it wouldn't have mattered if the Packers never won a single game—they held on to their season tickets and attended every game even in the 20-degree days that are all too common in Green Bay.

But then there are fair-weather fans, those who do not really identify with the team on a deep level. What happens when their team gets clobbered? They distance themselves from the team. They don't show up to games, they don't wear their team T-shirts. They may even find a new team to identify with. Why? Because rooting for a loser hurts their self-esteem. It hurts the esteem of true fans, too, but they endure it because they have to support the team.

When My Group Is Attacked, It Makes Me Want to Leave

Now I am going to extend this analogy to your racial or gender group. When people who do not have a strong identification with their group—fair-weather fans—are being clobbered, they jump ship to a winning group because it helps their self-esteem. Of course, it's completely unconscious. People do not say "I want to be less Mexican and more white," but they do start trying to see themselves as more similar to white people while also looking for reasons to see themselves as different from other Mexicans.

For example, in a research study scientists asked policewomen to recall a time when they had experienced gender bias at work. That required the women to think about a time when their gender group had been disrespected. Being reminded of that mistreatment caused the women to see themselves as different from other women; they actually de-identified with other women and downplayed the prevalence of sexism.[2] It's not just women who do this. The same researchers asked Surinamese immigrants to recall an instance of racial bias against their group, and doing so caused those subjects to de-identify with their group as well.

The problem is that when distancers are in a position of power, it often results in their becoming gender (or race) gatekeepers, such that they won't let anyone else in so that they remain a solo. This fear really stems from a zero-sum bias—the unfounded fear that if one person wins, another must lose. Game theory tells us that zero-sum games do exist. In such a situation, it might be rational to engage in competitive behavior. But most situations in life are not a zero-sum game. And distancing works to their detriment, as solo women, for example, are viewed more negatively than when women make up more of a team.[3]

THE FOLLY OF THE TEAM PLAYER

I'd never really believed that "women who don't support other women" actually existed. That's not to say that I'm not aware of the stereotype. All you have to do is google "bitchy bosses" to find hundreds of articles disparaging female leaders who don't help women because of their own competitiveness. But I thought they were boogeywomen created to blame women for their own lack of progress. I assumed that the belief in Team Players was just an instance of gender-role bias where we are particularly critical of women who violate their gender role.

In fact, the dogma promoted in the 1990s and early 2000s with books such as *Act Like a Lady, Think Like a Man: What Men Really Think About Love, Relationships, Intimacy, and Commitment*[4] or even the more recent *Lean In: Women, Work, and the Will to Lead*[5] essentially told women that success in the workplace could be achieved by their acting more like men. I cannot tell women *not* to act like men, because some women have very masculine personalities. What I can say is this: if your tendency is *not* to be hypermasculine and you decide to change your style to fit some masculine ideal (which is exhausting in and of itself), you should know that the data say it will actually hurt your performance. In some of my own research, I have found that woman leaders who act masculine without also engaging in more feminine behaviors (such as being sensitive and warm) are less successful leaders.[6]

Mary, a management consultant, told me about her experience in corporate America in the 1980s. She'd always been tough. Growing up the only girl in a family of eight kids had helped her get ahead in business and sharpened her ability to fit in and be "one of the boys," which was all but required in the 1980s office place. She wore the large shoulder pads and neckties that women wore in the office to symbolize that they were just as strong and tough as men. But her masculine demeanor could get her only so far. "As you reach the top of an organization, your job becomes all about relationships—and I did not have good relationships with other people." After hiring an executive coach, she learned to be more reflective about the person she wanted to be and started spending more time advocating for and mentoring other women. Team Players might succeed initially because they fit in, but in the long run, their inability to form relationships with other women, POC, WOC, and LGBTQ makes them seem scheming and interpersonally cold, which stalls their progress.

Am I arguing that this double standard is okay? Absolutely not. But I have seen that the path to success is tougher for women who adopt this style, so if it is not your natural tendency, know that you might be disempowering your employees while simultaneously hurting yourself.

For example, having interpersonal conflicts with other women cause women to be judged negatively by their colleagues.[7] And being a champion of white men often backfires against women, as Apple's vice president of diversity and inclusion, Denise Young Smith, an African American woman, experienced while speaking at the One Young World Summit (a UK-based charity focused on leaders making positive changes in the world). She said, "There can be twelve white, blue-eyed, blond men in a room and they're going to be diverse too because they're going to bring a different life experience and life perspective to the conversation."[8] She received such strong negative press that she eventually stepped down from her position.

THE MAIN MISTAKE AND MYTH AT THE HEART OF TEAM PLAYING

The Mistake of Letting Stereotypes Threaten You

The fact is that identifying with your racial or gender group when others view it negatively can hurt your self-esteem and even your performance. I was shocked when Reina, a Hispanic lawyer from Chicago, told me that she used to keep women out of her firm to make herself look good. Unlike most of the Team Players I talked to, she actually acknowledged doing it. "It was subconscious," she explained. "When we would consider hiring another woman to the firm, everyone would look to me, like I am the only person who was qualified to evaluate her résumé because I was a woman. And I would look at her résumé and I would always see flaws—maybe she did not come from the best school, or she did not have a lot of trial experience. And I would point that out. I might not have pointed out the same flaws for a man." Essentially, she thought that the men wanted her to criticize the women, so she did, and the men "responded positively when I was hard on the women." She also explained that she did not want everyone to think she was hiring a woman just because of her gender.

Her Team Player mentality changed following the 2017 Women's March and the rise of the #MeToo movement. She finally realized that if she—someone who had already broken barriers to become a gatekeeper—was not going to be fair to women, then women didn't stand a chance. The most important point that I learned from Reina was that women might feel as though supporting women actually reinforces pro–white man bias, compelling them to hold women to a higher standard.

Don't You Threaten Me

What is the psychology here? If women, POC, WOC, and LGBTQ believe they were hired because of their gender, race, or sexual identity, it hurts their self-esteem by psychologically confirming the stereotype that they are less competent. Essentially, it can create what the social psychologist Claude Steele calls stereotype threat, the anxiety caused when you are aware of stereotypes about your group and are afraid of confirming them.[9] Usually stereotype threat diminishes your performance, but it also hurts your self-views.

When you are the solo woman (or POC), the truth is that that fact alone creates a certain amount of stress, and when you add to that the anxiety caused by stereotype threat, such as how few women there are in leadership roles, it can hurt both your confidence and your performance. That was what I found in a research study that I started back in college.[10] Based on the idea that women know they are stereotyped as being less leaderlike, we tried to stereotype threaten women by showing them statistics about the lack of women in leadership roles.

Then we made them lead a group. That is so mean, right? When women were leading groups that were made up of more men than women, the stereotype threat manipulation diminished their confidence, increased their anxiety, and hurt their performance. But if there were more women than men on the team, the effect went away. One reason is that there is strength in numbers.

The Just-Because SHAM (She/He's A Minority)

This discussion comes up in so many talks I give on diversity. I hear it in my own department. We want to increase diversity in hiring. "But," someone chimes in, "we don't want them to think that we hired her/him *just because* she's/he's a minority" (the just-because SHAM). But why would she or he ever think that? Why wouldn't a person naturally think you hired her or him because of her or his awesomeness? Do white men ever say, "Man, I'm worried that they hired me just because of my race [or sex]"?

Thinking you were hired because of your race, gender, or disability can make you feel really bad, as one study showed. In a laboratory experiment, researchers assembled mixed-gender teams and assigned each one a leader. The leader was either male or female, and some leaders were told that they had been selected based on their gender. When a female leader was told that she had been selected based on her gender, she devalued her own leadership, took less credit for the team's success, viewed herself as deficient in leadership, and reported having less interest in being a leader in the future.[11] Men who were told that they were appointed to the leadership position just because of their gender had none of those outcomes.

I was giving a talk recently at the tech start-up SendGrid in Denver. I said that setting goals is good, and one woman in the back of the room raised her hand and asked, "If you set targets, won't people think they were just hired because of their race? I wouldn't want to get a job because of my gender."

I heard a great response to this from my friend Tara Dunn, the president of HighMark Law. She said, "Okay, if thirty percent of the time you *don't* get the job because you're a woman and thirty percent of the time you *think* you're only getting the job because you're a woman, and thirty percent of the time you really are not qualified, then you only have access to a tenth of the jobs out there. Just take the job."

Going back to the SendGrid story, I asked, "Why not? Just think about how many jobs you *didn't get* because of your gender. If someone is willing to hire you because of your gender—go for it! Would you let someone hire you because they were your dad's college buddy? Or because you used to golf with them? Those things are equally arbitrary reasons. I say, if someone wants to hire you for your gender, take the job and kill it. If you really did not deserve the job, you will prove it in your performance. But I doubt it."

The only difference between taking a job because your dad's college buddy hired you and taking a job because you're a woman is that there is no stereotype threat that people who "get advantages because of their dad's old buddies aren't competent," so people don't feel threatened by getting a hand up in that way.

An African American friend of mine, Jamie, told me a story like this. She said that in her first week at an elite college, a white student questioned why she should be at the college, saying that it "must be nice" to be black because it helps you get into school. She stared blankly at the kid, whose name was the same as that of the newly built gym on campus, only a few yards away from them. "Your family bought the gym," she said. "Do you think *you* got into this school based on your merit?"

Ironically, people see some sort of inherent fairness in the benefits received by the children of big donors or alumni when it comes to college. But what if you're a POC at an elite school? The idea is usually that you got in based on your race and don't deserve to be there—even though there may be no truth to the sentiment. I look at my own kids—if my daughter were to get into Stanford, I would tell her to go. I don't care if she gets in because her dad went there or because she's Mexican or because she identified a new species of parasite named the *Katelyneroia Johnsonia* (this has not actually happened yet, but I am kind of hoping it will). No matter how she got in, I would tell her to *go* and rock it while she is there.

Returning to my talk at SendGrid, James, a black man, responded to my "Who cares?" point by saying, "Black men also don't care if you hire us because of our race. Now, we do care when you *don't* hire us because of our race, but if you're willing to give me the job I want, I don't care if it is because of my suit, my wit, or my race."

I loved the words of Chanel, a black woman who worked for the government. She said, "Of course everyone is going to think you were hired because of your race or sex. Of course you are always going to have that fear. But does it even matter? You are going to be judged on your performance, so spend your energy on that and let the rest fall away. I am not going to let it bother me. The people who got into this position because of their connections or nepotism don't seem to care. So I am not going to let it bother me."

INCLUSIFYING ACTION: **Adopt a growth mind-set.**

How can you conquer stereotype threat? By adopting a growth mind-set. In her excellent book *Mindset: The New Psychology of Success*, Carol Dweck explained that a growth mind-set is a belief that talent "can be developed through hard work, good strategies, and input from others" as opposed to a fixed mind-set, where people believe that "their talents are innate gifts."[12] People with a fixed mind-set are at a disadvantage because they don't see room to improve; they feel that what they are is what they will always be. People with a growth mind-set are confident in their ability to learn and improve, which leads to better performance and success. But Dweck revealed that although we might have a tendency toward one or the other, it is possible for people who lean toward a fixed mind-set to develop a growth mind-set if they decide to.

The concept is relevant to stereotype threat because stereotypes are threatening only if you fear that your group is less competent than another group. But if you believe that competence is not something innate—if instead you believe that all competence can be developed (the data support this perspective)—then it invalidates all stereotypes. That's why multiple intervention studies have shown that adopting a growth mind-set diminishes stereotype threat.[13]

How can you develop a growth mind-set? Dweck has the answer to that, too. Setting learning and development goals for yourself reveals that all traits are malleable and activates a growth mind-set. Think about the following questions.

GROWTH MIND-SET ACTIVITY
What are all of the skills I need for success in my job [or as a leader]?
How can I best develop them?
To what level of competence do I aspire?
How will I know I have reached that point?

The Myth That Solos Succeed

Does clinging to your role as the only woman or POC in an organization actually pay off? The research unequivocally says *no*; being a solo (sometimes called token) woman or POC actually decreases the chances of success of that token and causes others to take a more biased and stereotyped view of him or her. For example, a study of law firms showed that when there was only one woman in an office, she was overwhelmingly disliked and had a very low chance of success. In contrast, in law firms with multiple women, women were better liked and more likely to succeed. Being a solo can also hurt your self-esteem; think back to my research study on stereotype threat.

The benefits gained from a team's being diversified are also smaller for solos. For example, one study showed that in order to see a positive effect of having women on a board, at least three women needed to be present.[14] Once there were three women on a board, all of them felt freer to raise issues and felt more likely to be heard. When there were three women, there was a more supportive atmosphere in which the women felt more comfortable associating with one another. There was also a reduction in token-ism and stereotyping, meaning that the female board members were no longer assumed to speak for all women. Unfortunately, most boards have two women.[15]

Although successful women are often characterized as bullies, surveys show that 60 to 75 percent of the people who are labeled bullies at work are men and 60 to 75 percent of the people bullied are women. But the stereotype that women have to be bullies to make it to the top persists, and it does encourage some women to adopt that demeanor (after all, 25 to 40 percent of bullies are women and 70 percent of women report that they have been bul-lied by a female boss).[16]

In the workplace, bullying frequently manifests as hostility, usually involving some power differential—formal or informal— that gives the bully free rein to behave badly without consequence. There are many types of bullying, but two broad categories are direct behaviors (yelling) and indirect behaviors (ostracizing or gossiping about others).[17] It is difficult to overcome bullying behaviors—the bully usually has power over the victim—but having clear guidance on acceptable behavior at work, as well as a zero-tolerance policy for bullying behaviors, can help. As mentioned earlier in this book, some organizations have cracked down on this type of destructive behavior, such as when Credit Suisse fired the banker Paul Dexter because he bullied a male intern.[18]

> **INCLUSIFYING ACTION: Ban bullying and try giving.**

The antidote to bullying is giving. As Adam Grant said in his book *Give and Take: A Revolutionary Approach to Success*, you can combat your competitive zero-sum bullying attitude with generosity—by giving.[19] Grant showed that givers find more meaning in their work and are happier than nongivers are. Moreover, giving behavior will diminish the negative reactions people have toward Team Players. Of course, you don't want to seem inauthentic when you go from being a bully on Monday to being supportive on Tuesday. It might make more sense to address the issue outright. I'd suggest beginning by having conversations with members of your team about your leadership strengths and weaknesses, asking them which things you do that they want you to do more of, which things you do that they want you to continue doing, and which things you do that they want you to do less of. Questions like these open the door to creating a more trusting relationship and allow you the latitude to try out new leadership behaviors, such as trying to be more generous.

Chapter 9

LEADERSHIP STRATEGIES FOR TEAM PLAYERS

I think not supporting women is complete bullshit. As Madeleine Albright says, "There's a special place in hell for women that don't support other women." There's absolutely no way I would be where I am today without the support of mentors and people, both men and women, who saved me from myself.

—LIZ SMITH, FORMER CEO, BLOOMIN' BRANDS (INCLUSIFYER)

I have seen many Team Players who came up in their companies in the 1980s become Inclusifyers today. Whereas early on they might have felt the need to distance themselves from other women to fit in, today's workplace encourages women to support women.

I am reminded of former Yahoo! CEO Marissa Mayer's quote when she was the first female engineer at Google: "I'm not really a woman at Google; I'm a geek at Google." During a PBS documentary

Makers: Women Who Make America, Mayer stated that she was not a feminist.[1] She was also notorious for working long hours, eschewing long maternity leaves, and ending flextime at the company. But in trying to prove that she and her leadership style fit into the masculine culture of Silicon Valley, she distanced herself from other women.

In one of her more controversial decisions, she banned the company's popular telecommuting policy[2] even though people who work remotely tend to be more engaged, committed, and enthusiastic about their work, according to Gallup (as long as they work outside the office less than 20 percent of the time). She took only two weeks off work after her son was born, and after the birth of her twins she took less than a month off. She was accused of setting back working women at Yahoo! rather than serving as a mentor or role model.[3]

Has Mayer's perspective changed since Yahoo! was purchased by Verizon and she lost her CEO position?[4] Maybe. She proposed creating a private club for workingwomen and families in the San Francisco Bay area,[5] and she has recently invested in a family play space in Tribeca in New York City.[6] Maybe these behaviors suggest that she has become more of an Inclusifyer or has at least gained empathy for the fact that being a working mom can be a challenge for many women.

BATTLE FOR THAT ONE SPOT

Some former Team Players told me that they unconsciously believed that if another woman made it to their level, it would make them less special or they would have to compete with the new woman to be recognized. But if I give you more respect, does it mean that there is less respect left for me? Clearly not—and in fact, I would probably get more respect in return. If I, as a female professor, hire more woman professors, do I lose resources such as raises and leadership options? Or do I gain things such as potential new collaborators, more help mentoring PhD students, more new knowledge and expertise to add to my department? Zero-sum bias is often just a myth that encourages us to hoard resources.

Jane Miller, the CEO of Lily's Sweets and part of the team that created Chili Cheese Fritos (thank you, Jane), is not at all a Team Player. She is 100 percent Inclusifyer. When she was working her way up in big corporations such as PepsiCo, Heinz, and Hostess in the 1980s, 1990s, and 2000s, there were very few women at the executive level. But she saw a strange dynamic: if there was just one woman out of ten in an executive position, the junior women all aspired to that one job. Miller didn't get it. "Why are they all looking to the job that the woman has? What about the other nine?" she wondered.

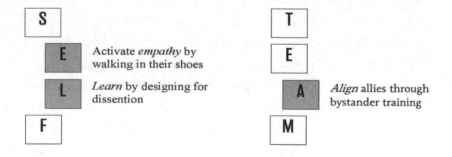

If you're a Team Player, you can move toward Inclusifying if you focus on the unique contributions that women, POC, WOC, and LGBTQ can make to your organization. You just need to increase your empathy by trying to walk in their shoes. In addition, you can focus on learning by designing for dissention and aligning allies.

WALK IN THEIR SHOES (EMPATHY)

Danielle, a human resources specialist in the health care sector, told me that she had grown up in a life of relative privilege: she came from a two-parent upper-middle-class household and had had a great college education. As she rose through the ranks of her organization, she never saw it as her job to support other African Americans. "I did not know about the experience of all African Americans; I only knew about my life experience, and it was not one that involved a lot of struggle and limited opportunity." Because she so easily fit into the dominant culture, it never occurred to her that others might feel lost or struggle in it. "I had not done the work to think about it," she said.

When she decided to find ways to increase diversity at her organization, she realized that her focus on equality—treating everyone the same—was not actually fair. "We needed to engage in active recruitment of African American employees who might not see themselves as having the skills we were looking for. They just needed to have someone tell them that they were the type of person we were looking for and that they would be welcomed in our organization." She did not know about systemic bias and implicit racism, but she became well aware of it by walking in others' shoes and was able to increase her awareness.

Team Players are usually out of touch with how other women, POC, WOC, and LGBTQ are feeling because they have distanced themselves from them. Therefore, they need to unleash their empathy to get back to a place where they can understand their co-workers' experiences. Because most of the Team Players I met were women and women tend to already be skilled in the art of empathy, I suggest that you take the time to follow the lesson *Walk in Their Shoes*.

Because of the psychological bias called *projection*, we all assume that everyone sees the world the same way that we do, and we project the most onto those who are the most similar to us. For example, when I interview women about sexual harassment, those who haven't been sexually harassed find it more difficult to believe that other women have been harassed. Basically, they believe that if it did not happen to them, it could not be happening to others. This inability to walk in other people's shoes makes it difficult to experience compassion for people who have had different experiences from yours. People who lack empathy tend to be judgmental of others who have had different experiences or have made choices different from their own. If you never consider other people's perspectives or look at things from their point of view, their choices can just seem wrong.

How to Create Empathy

Creating empathy is as simple as talking to people to try to learn about and understand their perspective. But if you don't typically walk around trying to learn about other people, it sometimes takes a jolt to make it happen. At least, that is what Samantha Gilbert, the Ford Foundation's vice president for talent and human resources, told me. The Ford Foundation was established by Edsel Ford with the goal of advancing human welfare around the world. I am a particular fan of it because I was awarded a Ford Foundation grant to fund my dissertation research.

Because the foundation started in 1936, there were old ways of doing things that had not caught up to the realities of the twenty-first century. Gilbert recognized the need to do so and hired a consultant to come in and do a culture audit. One of the consultant's recommendations was to increase conscious empathy by asking the following questions of people on the team:

Tell me about when you feel included.
- What makes you feel that way?
- How can we teach people to do more of that behavior?

Now, tell me about when you don't feel included.
- What makes you feel that way?
- How can we teach people to do less of that behavior?

Of course, you can't just ask questions; you also have to listen to the answers. Doing so will help increase your empathy.

DESIGN FOR DISSENSION (LEARN)

Another step toward making diversity and inclusion the foundation of a team is to ensure that you are listening to people who voice different opinions. The importance of open communication is summarized in Napoleon Bonaparte's statement: "The people to fear are not those who disagree with you, but those who disagree with you and are too cowardly to let you know."

Leaders can focus on learning from team members by *Designing for Dissension*. This will create structural mechanisms that facilitate the healthy communication of different viewpoints. Although this skill is good for any leader, *Designing for Dissension* is a great way to start changing the culture if you are a Team Player.

Once a good meeting environment is created, the next step is making sure everyone contributes so you don't miss out on important information. It could be creating a physical space that encourages interaction and reduces power dynamics, such as seating people in a circle. I also advocate for putting away technology (laptops, phones) unless needed for something specific. Dave Lougee, the CEO of the media giant Tegna, explained how information can be lost if you don't design for dissension.

Many years ago, Lougee attended leadership development training at the Center for Creative Leadership in Colorado Springs. A few days into the training the leaders did one of those wilderness survival activities where you rank the survival value of various items as an individual and then again as a group. If you google *lost in the wilderness team building exercise* you can find a long list of these—lost at sea, in outer space, in the desert, or in the snow. In this case, they were lost in the snowy mountains.

He recalls, "There were sixteen men and two women in the group. One was type A, like the sixteen men, and the other woman was more of the quiet, type B type. I remember when we first sat down to get to know each other, the type B woman talked about her hobby of mountaineering. I remember this clearly because she did not say much else." But when they divided into three teams, Lougee was not lucky enough to end up on the same team as the mountaineering outdoorswoman.

The group interactions were taped. During the debrief they learned that, overwhelmingly, the groups performed better than the individuals but one individual stood out as having the best performance, the quiet outdoorswoman. Yet her group performed the worst. What happened? When they watched the tape of the interaction the five other type A men on her team were mortified to see themselves dismiss her ideas, talk over her, and fail to even make eye contact with her.

Lougee explained, "I learned two equally profound lessons that day. First, as long as you have diverse perspectives, groups outperform individuals to a staggering degree. This is the wisdom of the crowd. Second, the person with the best ideas is not always heard, to the detriment of the team. As a leader you can't know what you don't hear, so you need to create strategies to get everyone to contribute—and that means increasing inclusion."

Why So Quiet?

But why don't people just naturally participate in meetings? They may lack confidence, think their perspective is not valued, or feel that they are talked over and their ideas are ignored. And sometimes they have been told directly to keep quiet. I remember going to a faculty meeting at one of my first jobs and sharing my thoughts on a few topics. After the meeting, a female faculty member pulled me aside in the hall to tell me that assistant professors (professors without tenure are called assistants) don't really *talk* during meetings. "Then why would I go?" I asked.

And it is not just me. A female friend of mine called me to seek some advice on how she is supposed to contribute at meetings. I will call her Kerry. Kerry worked at a large beverage manufacturer and had recently been promoted to a new position that gave her access to some executive-level meetings. She was a little nervous at the first meeting she attended and decided to just watch and listen to learn the social norms of the group. As she walked out through the tall frosted-glass doors of the conference room, she was pulled aside by a female executive, who told her that if she was not going to contribute to the discussion, she should not attend future meetings. So the next time around, she chimed in a couple of times and was feeling good about it. But after the meeting, the same female executive who had offered her advice before told her that if she had nothing important to say, she should go back to not speaking.

Neither of these examples is really about diversity, but they help explain why it might be difficult to get people to share their ideas.

Cultural norms or expectations can make people afraid to contribute or even more afraid *not* to contribute. If you want to maximize the benefits of diversity, the idea is to get people to contribute equally (as Google found in Project Aristotle[7]) while being sensitive to your team members' emotional needs so they can feel safe while sharing their thoughts. This might be all the more important for women, POC, WOC, and LGBTQ.

Make the Workplace Safe

Encouraging everyone to contribute requires creating what Harvard Business School leadership and management professor Amy Edmondson calls psychological safety, which is making people feel that they can take emotional or relational risks in the organization.[8] Not surprisingly, Edmondson and her colleagues find that inclusive leader behaviors that primarily involve the leader learning from others (encouraging followers to take initiative, asking for the input of team members, and valuing the opinion of others equally) were positively related to team members' psychological safety.[9] And if you want to capitalize on the benefits of diversity, you need to create a safe environment in which everyone can contribute.

I have heard many other great communication strategies for designing for dissension. At the simplest level, it could be having a rule of no interruptions because women, some minority groups, and introverts may feel less comfortable about interrupting. It could be requiring that people think about ideas ahead of time and take turns sharing their ideas during meetings to avoid the put-on-the-spot feeling that less assertive people sometimes have. One employee raved about his boss's skill in designing for dissension and ensuring that one individual never dominates the conversation.

He might say, "Hey, [John], I just want to give you a heads-up. In a couple of minutes, I'm going to call on you on this particular topic." That gives John a chance to get his thoughts into order so that when he does speak in a couple of minutes, it's not just off the top of his head, which again creates inclusion and consequently elicits better thought processes.

Devil's Advocate in a Catholic Hospital

Inclusifyer Kevin E. Lofton, the CEO of CommonSpirit Health and former CEO of Denver-based Catholic Health Initiatives, shared with me his practice of encouraging diversity in decision-making in meetings to help create the best outcomes: he appoints a "devil's advocate" at every meeting, which is a bold move in a faith-based organization in which getting along with one another feels like a cultural imperative. "I want to show people that I am serious about wanting different ideas. And I want those ideas to be tested, whether they are mine or someone else's. What's important is that people know that they are not going to step on toes when they are doing it. No one is going to lose face if an idea doesn't work or if someone who questions an idea doesn't have a leg to stand on. That could just open the door for another idea to enter, and maybe we get more innovation that way."

Leaders who want participation in meetings almost universally offer praise for different ideas and ensure that the conversation remains respectful. Another great tool is to summarize the points made at the end of the meeting and ask if anything was omitted or if others had ideas to add. You can also force people to argue the opposite of their opinion to highlight the holes in their position. In all cases, the goal is to find a way to encourage people to speak up and create an environment in which everyone can be heard.

Ways to Design for Dissension

- Create a rule that interruptions are not allowed.
- Appoint a devil's advocate.
- Send questions to meeting attendees in advance.
- Have everyone share his or her ideas.
- Praise people for raising dissenting ideas.
- Let people know in advance that you are going to call on them.
- Ask people to argue for the viewpoint opposing their own.
- Positively reinforce contributions.
- Ensure that disrespectful comments are not accepted.

Creating a sense of safety does take some work on the part of the leader, but the payoff in creativity, camaraderie, and trust is worth it.

ALIGN ALLIES THROUGH BYSTANDER TRAINING (ALIGN)

One very effective intervention to align everyone to work for a common cause is through bystander intervention training. It works on the assumption that there are many organizational members who share Inclusifyed values and would willingly participate in efforts to reduce harassment, discrimination, and bullying; they just don't know how. Team Players are well connected to the majority group members in the office and can bring them in to start a training like this.

When #MeToo began, many reporters asked me (as an expert on sexual harassment) how it was possible that offenders such as the former movie producer Harvey Weinstein and former host of the NBC *Today* show Matt Lauer could have engaged in egregious harassment behavior without anyone noticing. Or if others had noticed, why hadn't they done anything?

The Bystander Effect

I explained that so many people had been aware of the harassment and witnessed it that it had actually made them less likely to step in. This was due to the so-called bystander effect. In fact, a classic study by the social psychologists John M. Darley and Bibb Latané showed that people are particularly unlikely to step in when they are part of a crowd because they don't feel the weight of responsibility. If no one else is doing anything, it sends a clear message that they themselves should not act.

In Darley and Latané's study, a student sat in one booth to discuss a topic with people in another booth.[10] They spoke to either one person or four people. Then another participant (who was actually in on the study) faked having a seizure. When there was only one participant, he or she stepped in to help 85 percent of the time. But when there were four participants, only 31 percent of people stepped in to help—not because those in that group didn't have a conscience but because each assumed that one of the others would act first.

Another of their studies showed that people will stay in a room that is filling with smoke if others in the room don't react.[11] Essentially, when we see that no one else is reacting, it sends a message that:

- Everything must be okay.
- The situation is not that bad.
- I shouldn't help because no one else is.

Especially in ambiguous situations, we look at others' behavior to tell us what to do. That's where Inclusifyers can have a big impact. One of the things that Inclusifyers do is set clear expectations for everyone about what behavior is appropriate and what to do when you observe inappropriate behavior.

One of the few tools that have been proved effective in combating negative workplace behaviors, such as sexual harassment and bullying, is bystander intervention training.[12] It teaches people how to step in if they see a problem, aligning everyone by having white men also join in as part of the solution to diversity.

Bystander intervention training teaches people how to:
- Notice events and label them as a problem;
- Feel motivated, capable, and empowered to step in;
- Have a plan for what to do and actually do it.

The question is, what type of events do they need to look for?

The most common types of bystander intervention training relate to sexual harassment, discrimination, and bullying.

Sexual Harassment Behaviors
- Offers of employment benefits in exchange for sexual favors or threats if they are not given
- Sexual assault, including touching or groping
- Requests for sexual favors or unwanted sexual advances
- Exposing oneself or showing photos with nudity
- Making explicit comments about another person in the office
- Making jokes about sexual acts or a person's sexual orientation
- Discussing one's sexual experiences or fantasies at work

Discrimination
- Limiting one's options for employment or advancement based on a protected status (race, sex, sexual orientation, disability, age, national orientation)
- Making negative comments about people based on a protected status
- Making negative comments about people's protected status to them (e.g., "All men are jerks")
- Making jokes about a protected status
- Negative nonverbal behavior aimed at someone with a protected status

Bullying
- Spreading rumors about someone
- Physically intimidating someone
- Making fun of someone's appearance or other trait
- Publicly humiliating or degrading someone
- Making negative comments to someone (and then pretending they were a joke)
- Giving someone the silent treatment
- Excluding someone from social interactions

The next major question is, what should a bystander do to intervene? There are four options for what to do if you witness inappropriate behavior. I call this the DARE model.

Distract the perpetrator by interrupting the situation. You can ask to speak with the perpetrator, pull the target out of the situation, or change the topic.

Address the behavior of the perpetrator. If you feel comfortable addressing the behavior by confronting the perpetrator, you can do so in the moment ("Hey, cool it!") or you can pull the perpetrator aside ("Can I speak with you privately?"). Perhaps instead of berating or challenging the perpetrator—a common impulse—you can try to lead that person to see how his or her behavior is harmful with questions such as "Do you know how that sounded?" "What did you mean?" or "What was your goal in saying that?"

Recruit others to help. If you don't feel that you can handle the situation due to power differences or fear of repercussions, speak with a manager, human resources specialist, or other employees to gain strength in numbers.

Engage the target in conversation. Ask questions about how the person felt in the situation. Rather than starting with "You are being harassed/bullied," explain that you witnessed a situation that you found inappropriate but want to know how the target feels about it. Ask "Are you comfortable with the situation?" or "How are you feeling about what happened?" Then offer your help. Most important, explain that it is not his or her fault.

Many people perceive bystander intervention training as a way of policing men. But in reality, it is equally as effective at limiting women's bullying behaviors.[13] What is most important is to reinforce to the team that these behaviors are getting in the way of the team meeting its goals and that the training is designed to help ensure that the team is as engaged, productive, and effective as possible.

Chapter 10

WHITE KNIGHT

When *He Doesn't* Save the Day

EXEC: *Women, they are people managers, right? Women empathize more, understand people better, engage in dialogue. That's going to be good, right . . . it can only be good, right?*
ME: *Is your team pretty gender diverse?*
EXEC: *No, we're all men. We used to have a female, which I loved. She left me.*
—SENIOR EXECUTIVE, RESEARCH AND DEVELOPMENT

WHITE KNIGHT: ORIGINS

Many little girls and boys learn to love the idea of a knight in shining armor saving a princess. Some of those girls and boys grow up and need saving, and some grow up wanting to save others. Last summer we borrowed our neighbors' kayaks for a lake trip. When we got back, I saw our neighbor doing some work on his car and shouted that I would bring the kayaks over. He responded, "We don't need them now—you can wait for your husband to bring them." Overhearing the conversation, my husband popped out of the garage, saying, "Stef's got it—she's hardy." "Chivalry is dead," said the neighbor.

The behaviors we associate with chivalry that are commonly instilled in young men—such as respectfully holding the door for a woman or carrying her luggage, and treating women differently from, even better than, men—are often taught to us by our parents. If all of those ideals feel right to you and you carry them into the office, it sometimes manifests as White Knighthood. White Knights have the best of intentions in supporting and promoting women (and minorities—but most often women) because they recognize the inequities that women face in the workplace and they want to help rectify them. But if you notice that your efforts to lift up women are not resulting in their upward mobility, or you experience a certain level of backlash from other men in the office, it's possible that you're coming off as more of a White Knight than an Inclusifyer.

Importantly, a chivalrous White Knight needs a damsel in distress. Many women I have spoken with enjoyed being protected by White Knights and accept and even encourage being treated differently from men. They see this behavior as respectful. The thing about social roles is that they affect both men and women. Living in Colorado, I sometimes forget this idea, but on a recent trip to share my research with a women's group in the South, I interviewed a few women about leadership and it was brought home to me.

One of those interviews was over lunch, where a woman, Savannah, shared with me a horror story of going on a business trip to Colorado. She said she had approached the table and been taken aback when no one arose to greet her. It was clear that no one was going to pull her chair out for her, so she pulled it out and sat down. She waited, her chair hanging out into space, for someone to push her in. "I just didn't know what to do," she told me. I said, "Well, you just sort of scooch yourself in, like this," and I demonstrated with my own chair. During the same lunch she explained that she wanted gender equality and believed in equal pay, but she still believed in basic values and expected to be treated like a lady.

So if White Knights want to put women, POC, WOC, and LGBTQ on a pedestal and some women like standing there, then how can a pedestal be bad?

THE FOLLY OF THE WHITE KNIGHT

The folly of the White Knight is not rooted in his support of women, POC, WOC, or LGBTQ; all of the Inclusifyers I met also supported and championed these minority groups. The problem is that White Knights' behavior can inadvertently send the message that those individuals are incompetent while also alienating other men in the organization.

Sandi Mays, the chief customer experience and information officer at Zayo, a fiber and bandwidth provider, is not the kind of woman who is willing to stand on anyone's pedestal. But she did find herself in the company of many White Knights throughout her career, especially as one of the very few women in the tech field. As she is one of the few Latinas I have met in Boulder, I instantly gravitated toward her when I gave a talk for Zayo. As I mingled with the crowd afterward, I could not help but notice the woman who dominated the room.

I asked her to coffee, seeking some mentorship from one of Boulder's most powerful women. We sat in a café in Boulder's Twenty-Ninth Street mall, me in my heels and Sandi in her trademark Ugg boots. She gave me great advice about navigating the labyrinth of career, family, and friendship. What stuck with me was how imperative it was that she had respectfully declined the chivalrous offers from White Knights along her career path. She said that they had just needed a little upward mentoring to see that she was not a fawn in need of help. She is a lion. And she let them know it before their fawn expectations could bite her in the ass.

"They always had the best of intentions—that was clear to me. I remember a time when the whole team was working on a project that was going to take all night. This was an important project. I knew that I wanted to be there, not only to help it succeed but also because I knew that everyone who worked on this was going to get some major rewards. It was just after six and we were all giving our dinner orders when my boss says, 'Sandi, where are your kids?' I looked around the room as if joking that I did not know where they were. 'They're fine,' I said. 'They're home with my husband.' My boss responded, 'I want you to go home. I know you have kids and we should not be burdening you or your husband with this right now. It's not his job.' I was dumbfounded and said, 'It is his job, though—my husband is a stay-at-home dad. I think I'll stay and finish out the project.'"

Like many White Knights, Sandi's boss was trying to be supportive and respect the importance of her work-life balance. But his belief that Sandi needed to go home to her kids, while the fathers in the room (there were no other women) did not, shows a clear gender bias.

Sandi also noted that the other men in the room rolled their eyes at her boss's words. "My boss wanted to support work-family, [but all] everyone else saw was another hour they would have to stay at work while I was asleep at home." She ended up staying all night, but the fact that the boss had given her an out was de-motivating for the rest of the team, who felt that the boss was play-ing favorites. And had she not declined, she would have missed out on a very important project. In this way, White Knights im-pede the success of women, POC, WOC, and LGBTQ employees while creating resentment among white men who feel that they are being treated unfairly.

But there is another unseen cost of protecting your employees. In the example of Sandi, her boss's protection could cause her—and those around her—to doubt her competence, creating a self-fulfilling prophecy. The White Knight's protective behavior ac-tually causes those expectations to manifest in a self-fulfilling prophecy. For example, one study showed that women who inter-act with helpful White Knights end up perceiving themselves as less competent.[1]

THE MAIN MISTAKE AND MYTH AT THE HEART OF WHITE KNIGHTING

The Mistake of Messaging Incompetence

The problem with the White Knight mentality is that it often stems from unconscious gender (or racial) biases that compel White Knights to protect women, POC, WOC, and LGBTQ. With regard to women, this often translates into a paternalistic view of wanting to take care of them like a child. I have worked with many senior men who have told me that I remind them of their daughters or that I am the same age as their children. In fact, studies show that men become more supportive of women in the workplace when they have daughters, probably because of that paternalism. But when you are thinking of a woman as a child, you can't see her as a colleague.

This paternalism, sometimes called benevolent sexism, which is a form of positive gender stereotyping, actually elicits pro–white man bias in disturbing ways. Just hearing positive messages about women, such as "women should be cherished and protected by men," "women should be set on a pedestal," and "women have superior moral sensibility," causes people to believe that women are and should be warmer and less competent than men.

Think about it: If you saw someone being treated in a paternalistic way, wouldn't you question her competence, too? If someone is being taken care of, you assume that there must be a reason she can't take care of herself. The research shows that even when women engage in simple acts of accepting help from coworkers, such as an offer to fix a computer problem, those women are seen as less competent and less qualified for a high-competence occupation. Interestingly, men who accept the same kind of help are not seen as incompetent because their competence is already implied.[2]

Don't Make Me Look Bad

Think of a coworker who is a woman. List five adjectives that describe her.

Now think of a man in your office. Do those traits describe him as well? For most people, at least one or two of the traits that are used to describe a woman coworker would include something about her warmth. It might be that she is kind, helpful, a team player, agreeable, easy to get along with, or emotionally intelligent.

But if you were going to describe a man, it's unlikely you'd use those same words.

In one of my own studies I found that, in general, female leaders are thought of as being more sensitive (caring, good listener, empathetic) than male leaders.[3] Think of the most empathetic *male* leader you know. It is kind of difficult, right? Male leaders are more likely to be described as strong, dominant, and assertive. These are all characteristics associated with strength or agency and make leaders appear more competent than warm.

But it is not just leaders; women also tend to be described as more communal and less agentic in letters of recommendation. In one study, just like for leaders, focusing on communal characteristics was negatively related to hireability for both women and men. This effect was found even when controlling for candidates' objective attributes, such as experience or success.[4]

So what can managers do? One simple idea is to try and focus on women's competence when describing them. To check yourself, you can re-say (or rewrite) a comment about a woman using a man's name. For example, if you say, "Stefanie is a real joy to have around," try saying it again as, "Steven is a real joy to have around." If it sounds strange, then consider revising the content.

Not only does a White Knight's low expectations of women, POC, WOC, and LGBTQ affect how others see these groups, they can also shape group members' opinions of themselves. Essentially, if you don't expect a person to be all that capable, you treat him or her in a way that conveys that message. In educational settings, it has been widely shown, teachers often have lower expectations of POC (primarily Hispanic and black) students and therefore treat them as if they are less qualified. This behavior actually diminishes the students' self-confidence and causes them to perform as poorly as they are expected to.[5]

INCLUSIFYING ACTION: **Lift people up, don't carry them.**

When women receive paternalistic treatment, such as questioning their ability to handle situations by themselves, mansplaining a topic that they already know about, telling them how they should do their job, or carrying heavy things for them when they do not need help, it reduces their self-esteem and psychological well-being and increases their self-doubt.[6]

One marketing executive I spoke with nailed this problem, saying, "Some male leaders feel paternalistic toward their female employees. So when a female employee brings an issue or challenge forward, they jump in and try to solve the problem, as opposed to helping that individual work through a thought process to solve it on their own, the way they would with a man. It tells women that they can't do it." The lesson to White Knights who want to be Inclusifyers is: lift people up—don't carry them.

You Can Do It!

I worked with an executive, Richie, who was a champion for gender diversity. As I was giving a presentation to the executive leadership team at his firm, I talked a little about White Knights. At the end of the talk, Richie approached me and said he was afraid he was a White Knight. He said that he had put women's names forward for position after position, but they were not getting promoted. I asked, "What makes you think you're a White Knight? Just because the women aren't getting promoted?" He explained, "I never realized this until you said it, but I think I'm treating the women like they are fragile. I really do want to take care of them and help them, but I think that's sending the wrong message to the bosses, who are not taking them seriously."

I suggested doing a pivot if he really wanted to get the women promoted. I told him to sit down and think through the major job experiences the women would need in order to get promoted, then come up with a plan and a time line for how they can prepare themselves for the next move up. Finally, he should share the plan with "the bosses" so they have the women on their radar.

"No one is going to promote a woman because you tell them to; you need to *show* them how qualified she is," I explained.

Richie got in touch with me months after our meeting to tell me two things. One, that the women loved getting tougher assignments because it helped them learn, and two, that getting those assignments showed them that their boss really believed in them, which boosted their confidence even more.

So what is the take-home message? Focus on women's competence rather than their warmth. And definitely do this when you are talking about them in front of other people!

The Myth That Mentoring Means Down

Research confirms that when women are mentored by men, they garner more success in terms of salary and promotions and feel more satisfied with their career trajectory.[7] On the flip side, male mentors may send the message to others that women, POC, WOC, and LGBTQ need a champion to rescue them. In fact, the word *mentor* originated in Greek mythology, referring to an all-knowing guide who protected the weak, and we still think of mentors as protective today. But as White Knights work to Inclusify, they can adopt a more modern view of mentoring, that of a reciprocal relationship where mentor and mentee learn from each other.

The Trafton Train

I learned this lesson from Inclusifyer Gordon Trafton, a retired senior vice president of Canadian National Railway. He believes that mentoring should be much more of a two-way street. Trafton explains that so much of his career was affected by mentors that he saw a need for more mentoring at his alma mater, the Leeds School of Business at the University of Colorado Boulder (where I work). So Trafton started a mentoring program in the school and currently serves as a mentor to many students.

Of course, Trafton has a great deal of wisdom to share with students, but what really stands out to me is that he always describes his mentoring relationships as "reciprocal." In other words, he says that he learns as much from the students—many of whom are women, POC, WOC, and LGBTQ—as they learn from him. "I get the chance to increase my perspective," he explained. "To be fair, I will never know what it feels like to be a black woman in business school, but I have a little more insight into their experiences than I used to, and that helps me be a better mentor and a better person."

Interestingly, Trafton is not the only one who approaches mentoring this way. Many of the Inclusifyers I interviewed told me that mentoring is rewarding not just for the good feeling of helping others but also for the benefit of learning more about the lives of others who are different from them. It increases empathy and perspective, which gets you two steps closer to Inclusifying. As Liz Wiseman explained in *Rookie Smarts: Why Learning Beats Knowing in the New Game of Work*, senior people can learn a lot from rookies because rookies are not yet set in their ways, which means they are much more open to new, creative ways of doing things.[8]

Jed and Ted

A former Leeds student told me of his reciprocal mentoring relationship with a computer engineer in his office. Jed, the alum, is an artist. He is creative, outgoing, and energetic. But in his job he needs to work with engineers, who turn his art into graphics. He ended up in a reciprocal mentoring relationship with one of the engineers, Ted, whom he described as highly introverted. "I was trying to learn more about the technical side from this young guy, but I ended up really clueing into my self-awareness. I'm the kind of person who tends to dominate a conversation, anyway, but I can't do that with Ted. I have to really focus on controlling my extroversion and listening to him. At the same time, I think hanging out with me has taught him to let loose a little and learn a bit more about the business side. It is a perfect win-win."

What is interesting about the situation is that if Jed had directly asked Ted if he could mentor him, Ted would have never accepted him. He'd have been too shy. "If I had gone up to this guy and said, 'Hey, can I be your mentor?' I guarantee he would have said no. And if someone told me, 'This young engineer is going to mentor you,' I am sure I would have refused. But instead, I went up to him and said, 'Hey, there are things I can learn from you and I might have some insights for you, too . . . can you help me?' And this great relationship was formed."

INCLUSIFYING ACTION: **Try reciprocal mentoring.**

Reciprocal by Design

Importantly, reciprocal mentoring does not have to happen by accident. Many companies have recognized the benefit of this type of mentoring and launched programs to make it happen. In 2018, FedEx launched a reciprocal mentoring program where women from their employee resource group received mentoring by top-level leaders. The nine-month program has partnered fifteen mentors and fifteen mentees. The women's organization Catalyst[9] also works with organizations to help design programs to develop more talented female mentees and male mentors while creating better gender relations throughout organizations.

These programs solve a very real mentoring issue: mentor-mentee relationships tend to be pretty homogenous. It's estimated that 71 percent of mentoring relationships comprise mentors and mentees of the same race and gender and there is clear evidence that women, POC, and WOC receive less mentoring than white men, which can inhibit their career success.[10] But if mentoring relationships were framed in terms of mutual benefits, more leaders might find an interest in mentoring mentees who are different from them. If organizations structure this type of mentoring and mentors can enter the relationship with humility and a willingness to learn, the overall benefits can be astronomical.

Chapter 11

LEADERSHIP STRATEGIES FOR WHITE KNIGHTS

I give a lot of the credit for our diverse board to Marge Magner, who's the chair of the board. I have learned that when trying to solve for the future, you have to make sure the future is in the room. Define a problem, and empower the group to come up with solutions. It's not about me.

—DAVE LOUGEE, CEO, TEGNA (INCLUSIFYER)

While I was doing work within the green sector, I read a great story about an effort to plant trees in Detroit from 2011 to 2014. A local nonprofit, the Greening of Detroit, asked 7,500 people—primarily people of color—if they wanted trees planted in front of their homes. About a quarter of the residents declined, leaving the overwhelming question "why?" Researchers Christine E. Carmichael and Maureen H. McDonough were surprised by the outcome and decided to find out why it had occurred. They started by talking to the nonprofit employees. The nonprofit employees thought that the locals did not understand trees. One worker said, "You're dealing with a generation that has not been used to having trees, the people who remember the elms are getting older and older. Now we've got generations of people that have grown up without trees on their street, they don't even know what they're missing."[1]

The misperception that "they don't even know what they're missing" appears to be pretty rampant within the conservation movement, which has often characterized people as the enemy of the planet. Historically, many conservation efforts have involved White Knights stepping in to save minorities (and the environment) from themselves. For example, Prince William made a video about his conservation efforts in Africa that included only one black person (a child). This conveyed to others that the prince saw himself as a savior who was usurping the voice of the people in the region.

SAVIORS ARE COMPLEX

But as the late Clayton Christensen and his colleagues illuminated in *The Prosperity Paradox: How Innovation Can Lift Nations Out of Poverty*,[2] unless conservation workers connect with the people in the community to learn what they actually need and want—and involve them in the process—they run the risk of failure.

Back in Detroit, Carmichael and McDonough asked the residents why they did not want the trees. Did they not see the value in trees, as the nonprofit's employees had presumed? Their response was very telling. It was not the trees they didn't like, it was the people who had swept in to plant them without having engaged the residents first. They perceived the primarily white, upper-class nonprofit employees as taking a paternalistic view of the impoverished people in the neighborhood. As one resident said, "You know what, I really appreciate you today because that shows that someone is listening and someone is trying to find out what's really going on in our thoughts, the way we feel, and I just appreciate you guys."[3]

That woman's comments were similar to those of others in the study, who had felt disenfranchised when the environmentalists had never bothered to ask them for their input, instead stepping in to give poor people what they thought they needed. It is very easy to view others through our own lens and assume that we know what they want and need without even asking them.

This is the paradox that many White Knights face. Your heart may be in the right place, but to really Inclusify, you are best served by ensuring that everyone is aligned (the A in TEAM) through a process I call *Sharing the Round Table*. You can also improve esprit de corps by focusing on empowerment (the E in TEAM) by trying to *Pygmalion Your People*. Finally, it is important to emphasize fairness (the F in SELF) by *Cleaning Up Office Housework*.

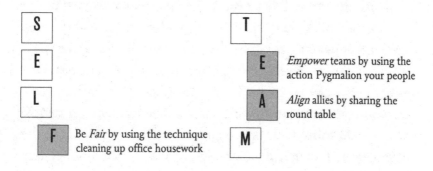

S

E

L

F   Be *Fair* by using the technique cleaning up office housework

T

E   *Empower* teams by using the action Pygmalion your people

A   *Align* allies by sharing the round table

M

SHARE THE ROUND TABLE (ALIGN)

King Arthur's Round Table was designed to show the equality among his knights. By eliminating the possibility for any knight to sit at the head of the table, the arrangement prevented anyone from being perceived as having any more power than anyone else. Remembering that image can really benefit White Knights. It requires giving everyone an equal seat and an equal say, including other white men! By sharing the Round Table, White Knights can increase alignment and build the TEAM.

Boston Consulting Group has shown that when men are engaged in gender inclusion programs, 96 percent of organizations see progress, whereas only 30 percent of organizations in which men are not engaged see progress.[4] So it's crucial to encourage majority members to engage other majority members in conversations around diversity.

The problem is that many white men don't believe that lack of diversity is an issue. For example, white Americans tend to perceive that the United States has made greater progress toward racial equality than do black Americans.[5] Similarly, men and women differ in their perceptions of the degree to which gender relations have improved over time. A recent survey of eighteen-to-thirty-two-year-olds revealed that a full three-quarters of women believe that more changes are needed to achieve gender equality in the workplace, while only about half (57 percent) of men agree.[6]

So what can or should be done to convince white men to work for change? It can be tricky. In my interviews with male allies— men who commit to advocating for women—many men told me that they had missed out on an opportunity to create change because they had alienated other men. Some of those allies were White Knights.

One man, Jim, talked about his approach to sharing his company's lack of progress on diversity. Though he had been trying to get his colleagues to help increase diversity and inclusion, all he had done was anger them. "I stood up in front of a bunch of directors, and I put up some statistics, and I basically yelled at them. I wasn't really yelling, but I mean metaphorically: 'We can do better!' And what I got—I mean, the immediate reaction in the room didn't matter—but what I got later was people froze up, because I was attacking. So I learned that it didn't work at all." So in the end they became less likely to want to support diversity and inclusion because they were angry at being disrespected by another man.

In so many conversations about race and gender bias, people call each other racist or sexist. Here is the problem: if you make someone feel attacked or bullied, it triggers the part of the brain called the amygdala, which tells that person to engage in fight or flight.[7] At that point, the part of the brain that enables us to think logically (the prefrontal cortex) turns off. The person literally cannot think straight. How far do you think you are going to make it in a conversation if the person you are talking to feels attacked? He is going to either fight back, even if his argument lacks validity, or flee the scene and say he doesn't want to talk to you.

The Benefit of Speaking Male

The reality is that we are much more likely to hear and accept a message from someone who is similar to us than from one who is different from us. This is not at all a diversity example, but I saw how powerful it can be to do a little grassroots communication. For more than a decade, I have worked with the Center for Construction Research and Training (CPWR) and the National Institute for Occupational Safety and Health/Centers for Disease Control and Prevention (NIOSH/CDC) to increase safety in the construction industry. To that end, I helped create a safety leadership training class to be offered as an elective in the Occupational Safety and Health Administration (OSHA) training course (called OSHA-30 because it is thirty hours long).

We thought that the difficult part would be getting OSHA to adopt the module, but even after we achieved that goal in January 2017, we realized that the difficult part would actually be getting people to opt in to the module. So we tried to find some folks who spoke male. We identified key influencers and shared the information about the project with them. Then we let them spread the word. Importantly, we involved industry experts in every stage of the training development: identifying key topics, creating materials, and testing the effectiveness of the training. The fact that the course was endorsed by people in the industry helped validate it, and an estimated 25,000 students took the course in the first year.

This idea also applies to spreading the word about diversity, as I learned from Wade Davis when we met at the *New York Times* New Rules Summit in 2018. Wade, a black, gay, feminist former NFL player, works to promote women, WOC, POC, and the LGBTQ community. "Men just don't listen to women. We should, but we just don't. But we do listen to other men." This is important because most of the people who are vocal about gender bias are women. If men are not listening to us, they are missing the message, even though they might be open to it if they were able to hear it.

Smooth Talking

Davis also revealed another benefit of having men engage with other men in conversations about diversity: they might feel less threatened. When men hear women talking about sexual harassment, one of the knee-jerk reactions is for men to defend themselves. They are thinking, "I am not a sexist or a sexual harasser."

So they are not listening to the problem, and they are not trying to solve the problem. They just want you to know that they are not the problem. *Not all men are sexual harassers!*

What a man can explain, without coming off as confrontational or accusatory, is that yes, not all men are harassers—*and* all women experience sexual harassment. In other words, men can flip the conversation to say that this is not about you being accused of being a bad person (or about you at all), it is about increasing awareness of bias. This is what the movement #YesAllWomen[8] has revealed. If white men don't feel like they are being accused of being part of the problem, then they are more willing to help find solutions.

Role Models

On top of the benefit of speaking male, men who are able to champion diversity without offending their colleagues can act as role models for how other men should behave. Professor Albert Bandura has shown repeatedly that we are most likely to learn from role models who are similar to us.[9] So when men support diversity, they are unconsciously teaching other men how to behave. This is sometimes called social proof: a phenomenon wherein people assume that others know the correct behavior in a given situation and therefore behave in accordance with the ways others do, especially those who are similar to themselves.

As Karl Preissner, the global manager of diversity and inclusion at Procter & Gamble, points out, "Men often look to other men to learn how to behave, so we need men to act as positive role models for each other." Using Catalyst's Men Advocating Real Change (MARC) training, the company empowers men to encourage other men to support women. The result? Procter & Gamble is one of the top companies for executive women based on the representation of women in executive roles, according to the National

Association for Female Executives. And Procter & Gamble's big suggestion for how male allies can bring other men into the fold is simply by talking to them.

As a final benefit of speaking male, men can help other men think about what it means to be a man, especially a white man. Like most women, WOC, and POC, I had never considered what it must feel like to be a white man. It was only when I met Michael Welp, a cofounder of White Men as Full Diversity Partners, that I ever considered an important question: "How can men understand what it is like to be a woman if they have never even thought about what it means to be a man?" Welp explains, "To be white and to be male is to not have to think much about being white and male. The world is set up for us."

In his work, a sort of diversity consulting mixed with self-discovery, Welp asks white men to ask themselves questions such as these:

- When or how have you thought about being white?
- When was the first time you interacted with someone who wasn't white?
- What are the cultural expectations of being white?
- Have you ever been told you're not man enough?
- How does it feel to man up?

By confronting their own identity, Welp finds, white men are better able to understand others' identities. Welp also points out that a disproportionate number of women, POC, WOC, and LGBTQ people dedicate their time to working on diversity, which in itself creates inequity. When men get involved, it lightens the load. It frees women, POC, and other marginalized groups from the exhausting work of coaching white men to understand their world. By being cognizant of uniqueness and belonging, we can work across cultural differences and come together to build powerful global organizations.

PYGMALION YOUR PEOPLE (EMPOWER)

In much the same way that having low expectations of employees can diminish their performance, having high expectations can increase feelings of empowerment, activating the E in TEAM. A positive instance of a self-fulfilling prophecy is called the Pygmalion effect, a term coined by the psychologist Robert Rosenthal to describe what happens when teachers hold high expectations of their students.[10] Rather than trying to save their team members, I suggest White Knights shift to empowering their team members using the Pygmalion effect.

In his classic study, Rosenthal told teachers that certain of their students were gifted, although the students had actually been chosen randomly. He found that the "gifted" students ended up performing better in the long run. Why? Because the teachers expected them to. They asked harder questions of them, made them persist on difficult tasks, and offered them more help.

Similar experiments on military leadership yielded the same findings: the cadets or other military personnel who were expected to perform better than the others did actually perform better, even though they showed zero extra intelligence or ability.[11] The lesson for organizational leaders is the same: rather than expecting women, POC, WOC, and LGBTQ to need help, operate under the assumption that they are gifted. Treat them that way, and it will become a self-fulfilling prophecy.

The Pygmalion effect usually means that you manipulate your expectations for one group over another. But in a study I did with some colleagues, we looked at so-called naturally occurring Pygmalion effects.[12] We found that leaders who had higher expectations of their followers elicited more positive relationships with and better performance from them.

Inclusifyers create this positive feedback loop for all of their employees by (1) thinking about what their employees need to do to advance in the organization and (2) giving all employees access to the tough assignments that will get them there. One study showed that White Knights who are trying to help with the best intention end up giving women (the study did not include minorities) easier job assignments. And without the tough assignments that create real learning, those women's success was impeded.

Pygmalion-ing your people is really about giving them their own voice and empowering them to take over their own career success.

When I interviewed Mary Barra, the CEO of General Motors, she told me how her bosses' high expectations had helped her reach her level of success. "I sit here today in the role of CEO because twenty-plus years ago, the leadership at the time in the company where I worked believed in diversity, and they gave me challenging and stretch assignments. They gave me constructive feedback to improve. There were many times I was appointed to a new position that I was not quite ready for. And people questioned me getting that job. But I said, 'I did not make this decision.' My boss believed in me, and it made me believe in myself and work all the harder to show everyone else that my boss was right."

CLEAN UP OFFICE HOUSEWORK (FAIR)

One way White Knights can actually increase fairness and enhance the SELF is by cleaning up office housework.

Interestingly, despite White Knights' desire to promote women, POC, WOC, or others, most White Knights I interacted with had not thought about the ways that office housework can weigh those groups down. Office housework includes non–revenue generating work that carries little risk but also little reward. Office housework can end up taking a tremendous amount of time, which is problematic because it does not lead to promotions for those who do it.[13] Take a wild guess as to who usually gets assigned those tasks.

Examples of office housework:

Parental Duties
- Cleaning up after meetings
- Planning parties and other social events
- Getting coffee/food for meetings

Secretarial Duties
- Taking notes at meetings
- Fetching documents during meetings
- Handling logistics and scheduling for meetings
- Keeping track of paperwork
- Keeping track of budgets
- Managing documents and data[14]

Service Tasks

- Filling in for a colleague
- Serving on a low-ranking committee
- Looking over someone else's work

In a study of lawyers conducted by the American Bar Association, researchers found that there are immense disparities in the types of assignments that women, POC, WOC, and LGBTQ are given compared with white men.[15] Women of color reported doing 20 percent more administrative tasks than white men did. White women were 18 percent more likely to do administrative tasks. More important, women, POC, WOC, and LGBTQ don't get any credit for these tasks. What's more, when men engage in office housework, they are rated 14 percent more favorably than a woman for doing it.[16]

There are lots of ways that women, POC, WOC, and LGBTQ can say no to doing office housework. But then they have to contend with the possibility of negative reactions or consequences. White Knights can solve the problem entirely by stepping in to ensure that office housework is distributed as equally as the highly visible assignments are.

One female accounting executive I interviewed said, "People come to a meeting, and somebody will say, 'Hey, can somebody take notes?' And as soon as you ask for a volunteer, it tends to go to a diverse candidate, is my experience. Because they're trying to make an impact, [but] they don't even realize that that act in and of itself is putting them in a [subservient] position. [Instead,] a leader [should say], 'Okay, we're gonna go around the room. This time it's your turn, and then next time it's gonna be your turn, and everybody gets their turn.'"

The rule is, if a task is nonpromotable (that is, it would never be listed as a reason why someone should be promoted), a leader should ensure that it is distributed equally among employees.

Chapter 12

SHEPHERD

Being Transparent with Your Flock

The boss is being inclusive of different cultures, but as a result I feel less included. There is a lot of Spanish being spoken, and I have no idea what they are saying. It makes me feel uncomfortable and excluded. But I keep it to myself.
—MIDLEVEL LEADER, GLOBAL DISTRIBUTION

SHEPHERD: ORIGINS

Shepherds are the female or POC correlates of White Knights. They support women, POC, WOC, and LGBTQ, but, unlike White Knights, they don't necessarily hold biased expectations of those they aim to help. Instead, their folly resides in how they are perceived by others. Essentially, they appear to be giving special treatment to people who look like themselves. Sometimes they are, sometimes they are not. Either way, it is the perception that matters, because when people feel that they are experiencing bias, they become angry and disengaged and want to leave their jobs.

You may have noticed some sideways glances from some members of your team if you are a strong female or minority leader who tries to provide support to other women, POC, WOC, and LGBTQ in a bid for diversity and inclusion. You may have had your promotion decisions questioned or received some backlash from white men. Or maybe you have never noticed any of those things but you have a sneaking suspicion that you are not as effective in the office as you could be. And now that you have just read this, you're starting to wonder if this is the reason why. If so, it is time to investigate whether people see you as a Shepherd.

Wanting to support other women, POC, WOC, and LGBTQ is no different from white men wanting to hire other people with "merit" (see Meritocracy Manager) or people who are a "culture fit" (see Culture Crusader). The only difference is scale: the fact that a few women in a company support the few other women is not going to create massive inequality because there are so few women (and fewer minorities) at the top of organizations.

Female and POC Shepherds turned Inclusifyers have learned to walk a fine line between championing others like themselves without appearing to give them special treatment. I know what you're thinking: "Wow, thanks, Stefanie! Leading from a tightrope sounds superfun." But many people do it well, and you can, too.

THE FOLLY OF THE SHEPHERD

Shepherds were difficult for me to identify because it was hard to pinpoint what they were doing wrong. When I first met the Latino leader referred to in the quote at the beginning of the chapter, he seemed like an Inclusifyer to me. I learned that he was a Shepherd only when I spoke with his white male colleagues, who felt that he was leaving them out. A Shepherd's weakness most often rests in not spending enough effort in managing others' impressions (although there are also some Shepherds who are truly biased against white men).

I saw the double standard turned against Shepherds at the Black Corporate Directors Conference in Laguna Beach, California, in 2017. One of the speakers, Taylor, told a story about pitching a venture capitalist (VC) to invest in his company. Taylor's entire pitch team was black, like himself, and one of the VC members commented that that was unprofessional. Taylor pointed out that the entire VC team was white. Why is it that an all-black team seems wrong but an all-white team does not?

Some of my own research demonstrated that there is a negative bias toward women, POC, WOC, and LGBTQ who support other women, POC, WOC, and LGBTQ. In fact, in experiments and field studies, we found that women, POC, WOC, and LGBTQ who valued diversity were seen as *less* competent and effective than those who did not and less effective than the white male leaders in the study, regardless of whether they did or did not value diversity.[1]

I remember when the African American former CEO of Sam's Club, Rosalind Brewer, said that she wanted to have more diversity at the table at Sam's Club. She was maligned in the press and called a racist because she wanted to support other African Americans, and Sam's Club stores across the country were boycotted. Such a backlash may be unfair and unfounded. Regardless, it limits Shepherds' ability to Inclusify. Shepherds need to be mindful of supporting all of their followers to the same extent that they do their female followers or followers of color. Shepherds might think that white men don't need support because they hold intrinsic power, and there are Shepherds who openly admit that they are biased against certain groups. But the truth is that we all need support and Inclusifyers support everyone.

Is it fair to blame Shepherds for the fact that others perceive them negatively? Obviously, the answer is no. But really, the point is not to blame any leader for his or her folly but instead to work to move beyond the folly to create more effective leaders and workplaces. The problem may not be a Shepherd's fault, but the end result is that he or she is not getting the most out of the team. Luckily, it is not too difficult to put some behaviors into place that will help Shepherds become Inclusifyers. It's true that some Shepherds out there really do, knowingly or unknowingly, give preferential treatment and unfair advantages to other women, POC, WOC, and LGBTQ, just as there are white male leaders who, knowingly or unknowingly, give unfair advantages to other white men. Maybe that's you, maybe it's not. Either way, the steps to Inclusifying are the same.

THE MAIN MISTAKE AND MYTH AT THE HEART OF SHEPHERDING

The Mistake of Man Hating

Imagine that you hired a new CEO who came into your office and said that he wanted to wipe out all the sensitivity in the office. He did not want girly vibes or innocuous femininity floating around. Everyone needed to man up and stop all of the collaboration and teamwork. Sounds absurd, right? But that was the message that many men I spoke with received during the workplace diversity trainings at Google that spurred an infamous Google memo.

The HR department at Google had handed out a memo instructing managers at the company on how to be "inclusive." According to a lawsuit against the company, it had advised them not to reward employees for traits "valued by the U.S. white/male dominant culture," including individual achievement and meritocracy.

VALUED BY U.S. WHITE/MALE DOMINANT CULTURE	COMMONLY INVISIBILIZED OR DEVALUED BY U.S. WHITE/MALE DOMINANT CULTURE
Front of the room, persuasive	Listening, raises up multiple voicess
Arguing, winning	Identifying multiple viable paths
Either/Or	Both/And
Perfectionism	Everything's a work in progress
Urgency	Sustainability
Numbers driven	Narrative driven (quotes, qualitative)
Growth in number, size	Growth in quality
Protecting others from	Valuing self-determination
Short-term payoffs	Seven generations thinking
Avoiding conflict	Conflict is productive/necessary
Giving feedback indirectly (about you, but without you)	Giving feedback directly (with you)
Individual achievement	Collective achievement
Seeing us as unique/exceptional	Seeking connections between contexts
We are objective	Everything is subjective
Casual, informal, off-the-cuff	Formal, prepared, thought out
Meritocracy	Holding systems accountable for equitable outcomes
Colorblind racial frame	Noticing race/color and any racial patterns in treatment

The document went on to explain "how Google managers can give feedback to 'women and people of color' as opposed to giving feedback to males and Caucasians." According to the lawsuit, the table on the previous page was given to employees.[2]

As a backlash against the changes, one engineer, James Damore, wrote a memo outlining how men were being treated unfairly at Google as a result of the new inclusion policies and suggesting that women are not competent engineers. Damore was fired, after which he then sued for wrongful termination on the grounds that he had been discriminated against for being white, male, and conservative.

It is easy to say that Damore was just whining, and, full disclosure, I wrote an entire *Harvard Business Review* article refuting all of the fake "science" he used to explain why women are incapable of being engineers.[3]

But here's the thing: white men make up a large percentage of the workforce, and to suddenly go in and say that their way is bad and wrong is going to alienate a very large group of people. They may not even believe in meritocracy, but when you tell them that the "white male" culture should not be rewarded, the likely response is going to be pushback. You can achieve the same goal— rewarding people for team-based outcomes—without denouncing individual success as a result of favoritism or toxic masculinity.

Stop Rolling Your Eyes

Now, I am guessing what some of you are thinking . . .

"Oh, that is so sad. We have offended the men because we want a fair workplace."
"I have literally had my ass grabbed at work, but I am supposed to be sensitive to the men?"

"So you're telling me that white people get so much privilege
that I can't even tell them they have privilege out of fear of
hurting their feelings?"

"Women have been dealing with this type of thing for years.
Now it's men's turn to feel uncomfortable. Too bad."

I get where the sentiment is coming from: a lifetime of being
subjected to racism or sexism or getting the short end of the stick.
But even though those supporting #YesAllWomen have experienced harassment and mistreatment (and minorities even more
so), we know that not all men are perpetrators.

Here's what we have to ask ourselves if our ultimate goal is to
create a fairer and more effective workplace: Does punishing
men create a fairer workplace? Does punishing men create a more
effective workplace? To both, I say no. It is not fair to treat people
like shit, no matter who they are. And it doesn't do any good anyway. I have had the greatest male supporters of women tell me how
miserable it can be to sit through a public flogging. And what do
men do in that situation? They just stop listening and fume.

INCLUSIFYING ACTION: **Think right and left—not right and wrong.**

Telling people that the way they approach the world is wrong
is never going to convince anyone to listen to you. It might feel
good in the moment, but it is not going to help you lead the best
team. Instead, try to come to an agreement by listening more and
talking less. People are far more willing to listen to your point of
view if you listen to theirs. But when we have arguments about
race or gender, the feeling is usually "You are *not listening to me!*"

We want to make sure our views are heard first because we
think that if the other person only understood our views, he or

she would surely agree. But if you are in the driver's seat of your own emotions and you reach a point in a conversation where you feel as though the other person is not listening to you, try asking them questions rather than trying to force them to listen, so that you can really understand where the other person is coming from *before* you try to provide your perspective.

A Difficult Conversation

When you find yourself in such a situation, you can slow it down before you get really angry and say:

"I think I am not understanding, can we go back a little?" or
"Clearly we are not seeing eye to eye. Let's start over."

And then follow up with some questions:

"Can you tell me your views?"
"How do you see it?"
"What do you think I'm not understanding here?"
"What would you like to see happen?"
"I can see that you feel that way. Can you tell me how you think
    that happens?"
"What could I do to show you that is not the case?"
"Tell me more . . ."

The important thing is to be open to the possibility that there is another story and your perspective is not the only one.

That is not to say that as a leader you cannot have preferred modes of team behavior, but you don't have to antagonize people to get the results you want. For example, tell your team that you prefer they take turns speaking because you want to hear from everyone, not because the toxic masculinity in the room means that women are not being heard.

Rather than trying to focus on an idea—"we want to stamp out toxic masculinity"—focus on behaviors. What are the behaviors we want to add to or remove from our culture? Anyone can change their behaviors—and you don't have to shame people to get them to do so.

The Myth of Reverse Discrimination

Although I don't believe in man hating, it is important for Shepherds to recognize the rampant fear that white men have about reverse discrimination. An Ernst & Young national survey of a thousand workers found that a third of all respondents thought that a focus on diversity in the workplace has resulted in male candidates being overlooked,[4] although there are no data to support that feeling.[5] They also think that white men are excluded from diversity programs and even mentorship and training programs.

One man I interviewed said that he had been passed over for many executive positions in favor of women. He believed that at least 50 percent of the executives in his company were women. The number was actually slightly under 20 percent, but knowing the real stats did not change the way he felt. He said, "The boss is being 'inclusive.' Whether that plays out in terms of opportunities? You see people who may have been moved up, and all of these people are qualified, but you can't help but wonder. The woman who got the job I wanted was also more than qualified, but you still wonder, is that [diversity] helping them?"

Why is this? The backfire effect shows that when people receive evidence that contradicts their important beliefs, rather than changing their opinions, they dig their heels in to a greater extent. They double down on the belief that was just "disproven" rather than deal with the cognitive dissonance of admitting they are wrong.[6] Cognitive dissonance is the uncomfortable feeling you experience when your beliefs and behaviors (or two different beliefs) contrast.

One research study showed this very clearly. In two separate experiments, the researchers found that male scientists evaluated studies proving the existence of gender bias as being of lower quality than female scientists did. The researchers then did a third experiment in which they altered the findings of a completed research study on gender bias to show that there was no gender bias. Half of the participants in the experiment were given the article showing gender bias, and the other half were given the same exact article with the results changed to show no gender bias. Incredibly, male scientists considered the study to be higher quality when the results showed no gender bias than when they showed bias.[7]

INCLUSIFYING ACTION: **Prepare for perception.**

An Inclusifyer's job, therefore, is to be aware of this possibility and address it to avoid fears of reverse discrimination, because when employees feel they are being treated unfairly, they go ballistic. In one of my favorite studies, a scientist gave capuchin monkeys a slice of cucumber for pressing a lever. The monkeys happily pressed away until the experimenter gave one of the monkeys a grape rather than a cucumber slice. The other monkey pressed the lever and got another cucumber slice. She looked shocked (whatever that means for a capuchin). She hit the lever again and put her hand out. No grape. She was clearly annoyed, but her feeling escalated to outrage when the other monkey got a second grape. You can see it in the monkey's eyes on the YouTube videos. She was thinking, "It's not fair! I did the same work for less pay!"[8]

One study of 1,918 people found that employees who perceived bias against them were nearly three times as likely to be disengaged in their work, twice as likely to feel angry at work, and half as likely to feel proud of their organization. Most important, they were about three times as likely to want to quit their job within the year. The total cost of losing a valued employee ranges from 90 percent to 200 percent of that employee's annual salary.

But what was most interesting to me was who felt they had experienced bias: persons with disabilities reported the greatest levels of bias, followed by ethnic minorities, men, women, and whites. Men reported having experienced more bias than women! Even the gap between whites and ethnic minorities was less than 2 percent. And the people who were the most likely to perceive bias were also the most likely to be looking for a new job.[9]

The fear of unequal treatment can actually have negative consequences for how white men treat women, POC, WOC, and LGBTQ. One study that was conducted shortly after the 2016 presidential election showed that among people who strongly identified as white, learning that nonwhite people will outnumber white people by 2042 caused them to become more likely to support Donald Trump.[10]

Another study of more than a thousand top executives at mid-to-large-size US companies found that when a female or minority CEO was hired, white male managers experienced a reduced sense of identification with their organization and became less likely to want to help their fellow colleagues. Not surprisingly, their unwillingness to help was particularly strong toward minority colleagues.[11]

What does that mean for Shepherds? That it is essential to get ahead of the fear of reverse discrimination.

Chapter 13

LEADERSHIP STRATEGIES FOR SHEPHERDS

I think that the differences are important, so I try to work closely with the men on our team to leverage the different thought processes, experiences, and perspectives that men and women have brought to bear. I try to look at it from an abundance rather than scarcity perspective. My success has been a shared partnership for leadership with the men and women that I've worked with.

—*EILEEN McDONNELL, CEO, PENN MUTUAL (INCLUSIFYER)*

When Jo Wallace was hired as creative director of JWT London, a major UK advertising firm, she was horrified to learn of the massive pay gap between men and women in the organization. She made a plan to "obliterate" the company's reputation of being an agency of straight white men. In doing so she sent out a very strong antimale message in the marketing trade magazine *The Drum*, in which she wrote, "If you're going to troll me as an angry, white, privileged man claiming that you're now at a disadvantage . . . please #CheckYourPrivilege."[1]

Soon after, the firm had to engage in layoffs, and five white men were let go. Angered by what they perceived as reverse discrimination, the men sued.[2] Of course, the company claimed that the firings were totally based on performance. But Wallace may have shot herself in the foot by taking such a strong anti–"pale, stale males" (her words) stance before firing the men. Since then, the agency has merged with Wunderman, where Wallace continues to work. Wunderman is much more diverse than JWT London was, so the merger may help JWT achieve the diversity it wanted in the first place.

But the question remains, could Wallace have approached the situation in a different and more effective way? She was certainly trying to support women, but you don't need to lift women up by putting men down. When trying to create a culture of inclusion, you cannot attack the opposite sex. Imagine if her comments had been made about women or people of color!

Like Wallace, leaders who are female and POC need to know that their behavior is going to be scrutinized extra closely. But if fairness is your goal, it's incumbent upon you to look inward to see if you have any Shepherd tendencies. In this chapter I will cover a few strategies to take Shepherds to the next level of leadership.

Shepherds need to ensure that they are not alienating a large portion of their team members (whether they be white men, women, or certain minority groups), and they can actually make their diversity and inclusion efforts more successful by involving white men (and everyone else). Many of the groups I have worked with over the last two years, including Billie Jean King's Leadership Initiative, have focused a large part of their Inclusifying effort on bringing white men into the fold as allies. Involving white men serves two purposes. One, it sends the message that the campaign to increase diversity is not aimed at pushing white men out. Two, without having white men working on this issue, we are missing out on diversity of thought. One of the first steps to take to get white men to feel like valued members of the team and draw them into the conversation is to make a genuine effort to elicit their thoughts and opinions. Despite the obvious benefits of having men involved, only 38 percent of companies say that men are engaged in diversity and inclusion efforts.[3] According to a large-scale study, almost 70 percent of white men don't know whether people want them to participate. So extend that olive branch, and bring them into the fold.[4]

To do this, you should continue to support women, POC, WOC, and LGBTQ through amplification. At the same time, it is important to check the optics and ensure that you are transparent with your team members. Finally, even though you do a great job ensuring that women, POC, WOC, and LGBTQ feel included, you need to use your empathy skills to listen to white men through the tool I call *Hear the Bleat* (see below), which is essentially listening to men's perspectives on diversity and inclusion.

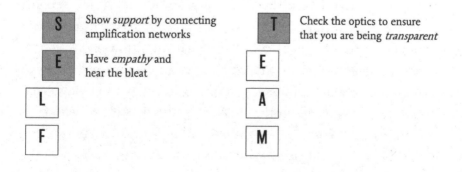

S — Show *support* by connecting amplification networks

E — Have *empathy* and hear the bleat

L

F

T — Check the optics to ensure that you are being *transparent*

E

A

M

CONNECT AMPLIFICATION NETWORKS (SUPPORT)

The first lesson, *Connect Amplification Networks*, helps Shepherds continue to support women, POC, WOC, and LGBTQ, but, rather than them doing it alone, it connects them with others to help support one another. I would never want to suggest that Shepherds stop supporting other women, POC, WOC, and LGBTQ. But instead of being the lone champion, I suggest that you share your supportive skills with your team members so they can amplify one another. As Ann Friedman's Shine Theory suggests, being jealous of other women, POC, or WOC (she describes Kelly Rowland's jealousy toward Beyoncé) is not helping anyone.[5] I think that is so last decade; the 2020s are all about women, POC, and WOC supporting and amplifying one another.

The idea of amplification draws from a strategy used by female staffers in the Barack Obama White House, such as Cecilia Muñoz, Anita Dunn, Susan Rice, and Valerie Jarrett. They had noticed that men tended to dominate meetings, so they started trying to openly support other women in meetings to help them shine. They did this by engaging in eye contact, echoing positive comments by other women, and reattributing comments to their original female source if a man in the room was given (or took) credit for a woman's ideas.

Amplification works by creating a vocal and visible support network for women, POC, WOC, and LGBTQ. I encourage women, minorities, and allies to start amplification sessions— essentially group support mechanisms—in which employees can share their thoughts outside the office, but they should also find ways to support one another inside the office. Anyone who feels as though he or she is not getting enough support at work can join the sessions. People can voice their concerns, such as "I cannot get a word in at meetings" or "The boss never listens to me," and other people will agree to help. It seems like a small thing, but when you are in a meeting and say, "I don't think anyone is listening to me," it sounds kind of weak. But when a colleague interjects and says, "I want to hear what Andreas has to say on this topic," it does not sound weak at all. And don't forget the white male allies.

Successful people I've chatted with over the years have told me that "the meeting before the meeting" is one of the keys to success. Influential people travel the halls when they are trying to get a vote passed or gain support for an initiative. They take the pulse of the group so they know who supports them. They try to convince people of their position one-on-one so the conversation does not get away from them during the meeting.

An amplification session is just another meeting before the meeting. It reminds people to support one another—assuming they agree—and creates a more level playing field for those who don't normally dominate the conversation.

But how can a Shepherd start holding amplification sessions? Employee resource groups (ERGs) are a great place to gather members in an amplification network. But if you don't have an ERG or you want to create a more diverse amplification network, I suggest organizing a lunch and talking about the idea while you are eating. In my experience, people love it.

CHECK THE OPTICS (TRANSPARENCY)

In addition, Shepherds need to *Check the Optics*. Even if there is very little truth in the idea of reverse discrimination, women, POC, WOC, and LGBTQ who support one another should take special care to combat this misperception. Essentially, the lesson here revolves around increasing team cohesion through aggressive transparency.

Even in cases where they were doing all of the right things, the Shepherds I spoke with did not see the point in public image building. But given that they are under such intense scrutiny, they should ensure that their public image is positive.

I learned this lesson from a corporate board I worked with early on. The board asked me to present on diversity at the company's quarterly board meeting. The entire time I spoke, a very conservative, older man with a finance background challenged me, cut me off, and even shouted at me. I will call him Jimmy. At one point he said he did not believe my data because I clearly had a "stake in this." I got pretty flustered. I had seen this before when the conservative radio host Rush Limbaugh had questioned a report on women and the economy by Suzanne Kapner in *Fortune* on the basis that she was a "chick reporter," but I'd never had to deal with it myself.

I wasn't sure how to argue with someone who just outright did not believe me, but I tried: "Well, I did not collect all of this data. This comes from McKinsey, the Pew Institute, Morgan Stanley." He was not sold. "I don't believe it," he said. "We are talking about money here." As if that were an argument in and of itself.

After my presentation was done, I sat down for dinner, still a little shaken by the experience. Had I really been so unconvincing? I know there are people who don't believe in climate change and even people who don't believe the earth is round despite massive amounts of evidence. So I guess there have to be people who won't believe the data on diversity. I went for one last drink that night in the thirty-second-floor bar of my hotel to try to make sense of what had just happened. My conclusion was that, knowing that even facts can be questioned, you need to find a way to communicate your information to a skeptic, rather than to people you think are open to your views. This means exploring both sides of every argument, presenting the counterfactual argument, sharing every data source, and presenting the details on how the data were collected. And even then there will be people who refuse to believe you.

What Can You Do Instead?

Checking the optics is really about (1) being aware of situations in which people might question you, (2) having transparency around your processes, and (3) openly sharing the data that helped you arrive at your solution.

I saw how checking the optics can help when I was inducted as a fellow of my major professional organization, the Society for Industrial and Organizational Psychology (SIOP). One of my female mentors, Mikki Hebl, who is a huge advocate for women, nominated me. To combat any implication of Shepherding, Hebl did her homework. She reviewed the publication records, citations, and funding records of the previous fellows over the past few years. She explained how she had found the numbers in a very transparent way so that anyone could go look at the numbers on their own. Then she shared the data in tables in the nomination letter.

When it was all assembled, my record, rather than my female nominator, stood out clearly. Female leaders and leaders of color need to take these added steps of transparency so they are not questioned by others. This does not just have the effect of silencing the skeptics; it also helps the beneficiaries of support feel more confident. At least, it did for me. Seeing my accomplishments laid out in black and white made me feel as though I really deserved to be there.

You Want to Start the Narrative

Essentially, you want to get ahead of one narrative before another is launched. I saw this firsthand when we developed the plan to anonymize the application process at Hubble. We started out with a survey of the astronomy community to assess their feedback. And we got some serious backlash. My favorite email went something like this: "Dear Sirs, I am not in support of the changes you propose. US taxpayers spend a lot of money on the support of HST. I believe that they expect, and deserve, to get the best science out of the facility of which it is capable."

Certainly, some people did not want to see a system changed that had benefited them over the years. "It just upsets the whole hierarchy—and what people are used to," explained one member of the review panel. Others thought the changes represented reverse discrimination. "Many of my colleagues and I believe Hubble is moving toward 'Guaranteed Outcomes' and 'Quotas,'" said one survey respondent. "The idea that scientific performance and membership in academic organizations must exactly match proportions in society is simplistic."

Clearly people were scared, which made it all the more important that Hubble be very transparent with its processes and invest heavily in strategic communication.

HEAR THE BLEAT (EMPATHY)

Because the major shortcoming of Shepherds is that they don't make all of their team members feel like part of the flock, they should work to bring them into the fold by trying to *Hear the Bleat*—the sound that sheep make to get others' attention—and engage in conscious empathy to ensure that they hear everyone's perspectives. Hearing the bleat requires having extra empathy for the perspectives of a Shepherd's outgroup (whether white men, women, or certain ethnic minorities) and explaining to them that you truly want to know if they ever have any concerns or issues that you can address.

As a woman or POC, it is easy to think that all white men fly through life on a magic carpet of privilege. But that is not the whole story. In her 2009 TED Talk, "The Danger of a Single Story," Chimamanda Adichie, a young Nigerian author, talked about the narratives we create for certain groups. As she put it, "The single story creates stereotypes, and the problem with stereotypes is not that they are untrue, but that they are incomplete. They make one story become the only story."[6]

I use this talk in my classes to ask students about single stories they have created for themselves or others. In my Women in Business class, I was impressed when one woman said, "I think it is easy for women to create a single story that all men have it easy, when in reality, they might have a certain amount of privilege in being a white male, but they could also have other headwinds that we don't consider."

Her comment stuck with me because in so many conversations about race and gender, I hear people grouping all white men into a single category ("white men do this" or "white men feel that"). Though we stereotype all white men with a single story, we expect them to recognize that women are not all the same: some may want to stay home with their children, some may want to run the country, some may want to do both. And minorities are not all the same: some Asian Americans might be reserved, while others may be completely different from this stereotype.

It made me think about the importance of having empathy for white men and listening to them in the same way we want to be listened to. This matters a lot. Leading effectively requires bringing everyone along. Even if certain practices are not meant to exclude anyone, if people do feel excluded, then your team is not Inclusifyed. I realize not everyone shares my views on this (see, for example, George Yancy's book *Look, a White!: Philosophical Essays on Whiteness.*[7]) In the workplace, in a leadership role, unless you work in a place with people who all look exactly like you, you need empathy to create the best team.

A woman named Dee told me about how she had found empathy for the men in her office. She worked in the masculine oil and gas industry and was one of very few women leaders at the VP level. She tended to feel steamrolled by the men in her office and often felt stereotyped because she was Asian American. "My team had men and women, and honestly, I found it a lot easier to lead the women. They seemed to listen to me more, and the guys had their own thing going."

To make matters worse, Dee had recently gone through a tough divorce and was feeling pretty down on men: "Between the divorce, Donald Trump, and #MeToo, I honestly started to think men were just the worst." When her employee gave her the book *How to Date Men When You Hate Men*,[8] she dived right in. The employee, another woman, had read the book and loved it, and the two talked about the book at the office—in front of their male coworkers—all the time. Dee passed the book along to another subordinate, and they all decided to go out for drinks after work to chat about it.

On a Sunday night, Dee went out for dinner with her brother Jim. He started telling her about his work woes. Apparently, some women in his office had a book club going, and they were reading *Why Women Should Rule the World.*[9] In Jim's view, the book focused on female superiority, and hearing the women in the office talking about it was making him feel uncomfortable.

Dee looked at her sweet brother, her face feeling hot with embarrassment over the realization that she was doing that exact thing to the men in her office, just with a different book. She told her brother to talk to his boss (another man) about it. He told her that the boss would never say anything out of fear of a group of women going into HR and calling him a sexist. "He told me, 'Men are just not allowed to confront women.'" This is a problem I will come back to.

The next day at work, she told her informal book club members about the conversation and suggested that they leave conversations about dating and hating men out of the office, and create a more gender inclusive book club if they wanted to keep it going. Then she made a plan to talk to each of the men on her team. "I really did not know what to say to them: 'Hey, man, sorry I talked about hating your entire gender, but it was all in jest'?"

Instead, she decided to be positive and try to listen. She told all of her subordinates that she was going to do a check-in. When she met with each person, she asked how he or she felt things were going at work and what his or her goals were. Then she asked each person to give her feedback: "Tell me one thing you would want more of in the office, less of, and what should we continue doing exactly the same."

The comments and ideas she heard from the men were great, and getting to know each one on a personal level helped her see that she could not lead effectively if she was engaging only with the women and letting the men "do their own thing." She was everyone's leader. According to Dee, those little conversations opened up ideas for ways that she could improve the office, do more team building, and have greater empathy for the men in her life.

But let's take this one step further. Because men might be reluctant to claim gender bias (like Jim's boss said), Shepherds might need to do even more. In the case of Dee, she also encouraged the men to talk to one another and come to her as a group if they felt that something was unfair. This way, she explained, no one person would be singled out for raising an issue. She would rather face an angry mob than lose valued employees who believed something was unfair but did not feel it was safe to bring it up. In reality, a mob never came—but her message went a long way to show the men that she was serious about wanting to hear their views.

Chapter 14

OPTIMIST

Positivity Without Action Does Not Get Results

Be yourself—you got to let people be themselves. And culture is big here. Diversity permeates our culture. You don't really need to do much because it's already here.
  —EXECUTIVE, GLOBAL SUPPLY CHAIN

OPTIMIST: ORIGINS

The Optimist was the most interesting find in my leadership research. I heard a lot of leaders talk about all of the great things they were doing to build belonging and all of their efforts to highlight uniqueness. They would use phrases such as "I want everyone to be their best self" and "I want them to bring their whole self to work." "I do things to build up the team. We had a Diwali party." They seemed to believe there was nothing left to do. But when I interviewed their team members, I got a different story: "I'm not sure if he cares about diversity and inclusion. I mean, he never directly talks about it." And: "I don't know if he really wants different viewpoints. I think he'd rather have clones of himself, but our team is diverse."

If you care about uniqueness and belonging and, as a supporter of diversity, you feel optimistic that it will happen naturally over time, you might be an Optimist. Optimism is a great characteristic and a hallmark of many entrepreneurs and successful business people. Optimists see the best in people and generally expect good things to happen. And when you hear statistics showing that women are outperforming men in college and 51 percent of the workforce is now women and there will be no racial majority by 2050, it is easy to believe that inclusive cultures will just happen naturally.

But time and time again, I saw that the companies that actually created change were those that were intentional about doing so. Marjorie "Marge" Magner has sat on her fair share of corporate boards, including those of Tegna, Accenture, and Ally Financial—all boards that are celebrated for their gender diversity. Whereas the average board has between zero and two women, Ally has three, and Accenture and Tegna each have four (although Marge retired from Tegna's board). The point is, she knows what it takes to change the status quo when it comes to board diversity.

She explained it to me like this: "It's not an accident when there are boards that have good diversity: diversity of gender, diversity of race, diversity of geography from a global standpoint, diversity of opinion. It's not an accident. Work has been done to accomplish that. The board doesn't wake up one morning and looking around and go, 'Wow, look at us! We're so excited that this just happened.' It takes work and it takes will to do it. And those who achieve it have made a commitment, and they reap the benefits of it." So rather than simply optimism, change requires action.

In many cases, the Optimists I talked to wanted to make a change but didn't know what to do first. In other cases, they were too comfortable with the status quo to want to change their behavior radically. If it ain't broke . . .

People settle in when they think things are working, so the problem with Optimists is that they lack the intention and motivation to initiate real change unless something triggers them to do so.

For Tim Ryan, the chairman at PwC US, the shift from Optimist to Inclusifyer started with the shooting deaths of two young black men in unrelated events in two different cities on two consecutive days. Before those events, Ryan believed in diversity. He had even done work in this regard in his previous role as vice chairman. But on July 5 and 6, 2016, in Baton Rouge and Falcon Heights, Alton Sterling and Philando Castile were shot by white police officers. Ryan choked up as he told me the story. "It just made me realize that something had to be done."

He had been chairman of PwC US only for four days. Later that month, he convened a meeting with other leaders at PwC, and they launched the idea for CEO Action for Diversity & Inclusion—a coalition that now has over 800 C-level leaders working to Inclusify their organizations. Like many of the other leaders whom I have identified as Inclusifyers, Ryan grew up relatively humble. A first-generation college student, he relates to the challenges people face in their lives. And he wants to create parity through Inclusifying. That means taking the risk of putting himself out there as an advocate and champion for diversity and inclusion, even if it raises some eyebrows and ruffles some feathers.

It feels good to be an Optimist because you can support unique-ness and belonging without alienating any group. It is also easy to be an Optimist because you don't need to put a lot of effort into making change; instead, you get to rest in the comfort of compla-cency. In other words, you simply maintain the status quo. You stay comfortable. The preference for doing the same thing because it's always more appealing than making a change is called the status quo bias. Think about the way you hired the last people at your organization. Why did you do it that way? Was it because it was how you had always done it?

THE FOLLY OF THE OPTIMIST

Almost universally, we believe that the way we have done some-thing in the past is a sound justification for continuing to do it that way in the future. Optimists are no different. It's just that instead of not wanting to change the way things are done because they don't believe in change at all, they don't want to change things because they naively assume that enough has already been done and things will naturally get better on their own.

As Voltaire wrote in *Candide*, optimism "is the obstinacy of maintaining that everything is best when it is worst."

It is a love of the status quo—thinking that inclusion is a natural state of being and that if they simply maintain the status quo, inclu-sion will happen naturally—that keeps Optimists from becoming Inclusifyers. One CEO I worked with who had a very diverse board assured me that inclusion at his organization had happened natu-rally "over the last fifteen to twenty years." You have to take small steps, goes the Optimist's thinking. It takes decades to make real change.

Only someone not affected by biases could possibly be satisfied waiting that long to feel included and welcomed. If you and your teams want to wait 170 years to have equality (that is what the World Economic Forum estimates it will take to have gender parity; it is longer for race), just sit back and remain optimistic. But if you want to see change in your lifetime, you need to start taking action.

As one man, Rob, from a professional services firm pointed out, the difference between an Optimist and an Inclusifyer is "pretty basic. Fundamentally, it's just actually talking about it. Actually engaging with their teams in the importance of diversity and inclusion. If you can't even have that conversation to help your team to understand the importance of diversity and you don't embrace bringing it into your strategy, then it doesn't get into the fabric of the team. But when leaders talk about it, the team understands its importance, and then the team feels more empowered to act."

His points are right on: talk about uniqueness and belonging and weave them into the fabric of the culture. The folly of the Optimist is thinking that maintaining the status quo is going to change the future. Keeping things the same is always more appealing than making a change. In his book *Predictably Irrational: The Hidden Forces That Shape Our Decisions*, the psychologist and behavioral economist Dan Ariely revealed how strong the status quo effect can be through his research on organ donation in European countries.

In some European countries, organ donation is the norm. In others, it is the exception. He explained that the difference between those countries is whether people need to opt in to donate an organ on their DMV form (check the box if they want to donate) or whether they have to opt out (check the box if they do not want to donate).

Ariely found that the type of check box makes a lot of difference—about an 83 percent difference.

In countries where opting in is the status quo—you have to check a box to opt out—about 98 percent of people donate their organs. In countries where opting out is the norm, only 15 percent of people donate. He argues that it is the way the question is phrased that influences the decision. If you believe that organ donation is the norm, you will assume that it is the right thing to do, there are no risks, and you will donate. If you assume that it is not the norm, you are less likely to choose to donate.[1]

The problem is that the same feeling of accepting the norm applies to making change in organizations with regard to uniqueness and belonging. Going with the norm feels a lot better than making a dramatic change or having to take a stand.

I interviewed with a company to do some consulting work about its diversity practices, and one of my first questions was where the CEO stood on diversity (in my view, the CEO is also the chief diversity officer, even if there is a formally named CDO). The human resources team I was meeting with said that he really cared about it but had not been personally involved. I asked what he had done in response to the recent violence against students of color in universities. It had been all over the news. They said nothing. He did not see events like that as relevant to the business. Note that this was a financial firm. They said that if there were an economic collapse in China, he would issue a press release but not for something like this. They asked what I thought he should do. I said I thought he should send out an external communication about how sorry the company is for the victims, their families, and the broader community affected by this tragedy. They thought it might be off brand. "That is never going to happen," they said.

Okay, plan B. I suggested sending an internal communication

to the people within the company recognizing that some of them might also be affected by those events and reminding them that there were support systems offered through the organization. They said he would not do that, either. He thought it might come off as political and that it might be off-message to potential shareholders or clients.

Would he send out a communication if there were a terrorist attack or a school shooting? Yes, they said. But not violence against students of color? I think that is terrorism, too, and not too far off from a school shooting. I informed them that sending a message would tell the company's employees of color that they are important, too—they are seen—and that the company leadership understands that such a series of events might affect them differently than it did white people. They stuck with no. I told them that I could not work with their CEO. When I arrived home, they called to inform me that I "did not get the job" and they were going to go in "a different direction."

THE MAIN MISTAKE AND MYTH OF OPTIMISTS

The Mistake of Confusing Equality and Equity

As a mom of two kids close in age (six and seven), I hear the word *fair* all the time. Most of the time their view of what is "fair" is getting the exact same thing. My daughter wants the same thing my son gets and vice versa. But it never makes sense to give them the same thing. They are different people with different ages, preferences, and needs, so, like most parents, I give each kid what he or she needs.

But as Aristotle said more than two thousand years ago, justice means that "equals should be treated equally and unequals un-equally." This means that if two individuals are the same, they should be treated the same, but if they differ in ways that are relevant to a specific context, they should be treated equitably. Paula Dressel of the Race Matters Institute says, "The route to achieving equity will not be accomplished through treating everyone equally. It will be achieved by treating everyone justly according to their circumstances." Here are some questions to ponder:

- If a woman has a hearing disability and you give her special headphones to hear clients on the phone, should everyone be given special headphones?
- If a man has back problems and you give him a back brace to do heavy lifting, should everyone be given a back brace?
- If a boy has diabetes and has to leave class to receive an insulin shot each day, should all the kids be allowed to leave class?

Of course not. All of these things seem absurd because the Americans with Disabilities Act tells us that organizations need to make reasonable accommodations for persons with disabilities who are qualified to do a given job. Equality is about giving everyone the same thing; equity is about giving people what they need to succeed.

INCLUSIFYING ACTION: **Choose equity over equality.**

For example, if an individual is addicted to nicotine, should he or she receive paid breaks to smoke? In fact, most organizations provide smoking breaks (about fifteen minutes long) several times a day, although they are not required by law. Why? Because they

know that their nicotine-addicted workers will be better performers if they get their fix. And yes, the workers are usually paid for
these breaks.[2] So as a society, we have decided that smokers should
get paid time off from work to puff—an average of eighty minutes
a day in some industries.[3]

But imagine if parents asked for paid time off to pick up their
children from school—say, an hour early one day a week (similar to
the amount of time spent smoking at work by the average smoker)
or two hours early three days a week (comparable to the high end
of smoking estimates). People would flip because it is "not fair."

- If a parent doesn't have day care one day, should he or she be
  allowed to leave work an hour early one day a week with pay?
- If a nursing mom wants to pump breast milk at work, should
  she be allowed paid pumping breaks?
- If a person's religious beliefs require that he or she pray several
  times during the day, should he or she be allowed to take paid
  prayer breaks at work?

Although organizations must provide pumping breaks to nursing mothers, those breaks do not have to be paid.[4] True leadership
is about giving people what they want and need to help them and
the whole organization be successful.

The Myth That When You Achieve Diversity, You're Done

Many companies have a diverse workforce but don't reap its full
benefits because they lack inclusion. Indeed, in a global survey,
one third of companies said that they are unprepared to create inclusion, while only 19 percent claimed to be fully ready to do so.[5]
In reality, inclusion (or Inclusifying) is the hard part, but it is also

necessary to get the greatest value from diversity.[6] Deloitte has shown that teams who have higher rates of inclusion outperform others by eight to one and that leaders have the greatest influence on inclusion.[7]

Deloitte has also found that people feel more engaged, empowered, and free to be themselves when their organization is inclusive.[8] It also reported that organizations are more innovative when they are inclusive. Only 10 percent of respondents saw their company as innovative when it lacked an inclusive culture, but in inclusive cultures, 74 percent of people believed that their organization fostered innovation. As a result, teams with greater levels of inclusion have better performance than less inclusive teams do.[9]

Long gone are the days of *tolerating diversity*. As Netflix's Vice President of Inclusion Strategy Vernā Myers has shown, diversity is not enough. In fact, my thinking on the topic has been highly influenced by her. Some years ago, I spoke at an annual summit on diversity that she assembled for the legal profession before she was a Netflix VP. She asked what time I wanted to speak. "Any time that is not right after you," I responded. If you watch her TED talk "How to Overcome Our Biases? Walk Boldly Toward Them," you will see that Vernā's speaking style is a confluence of charisma and emotion—she's not the kind of person you want to speak after.

At the conference, an audience member asked what to do with a leader who is trying to work on his tolerance but is not all the way there yet. She responded, "Let's start by throwing out the idea of tolerance. I don't want to be tolerated. You tolerate a nuisance. I want to be embraced." Myers's point is that we don't just want to be accepted *despite* who we are, we want to be accepted *because* of who we are and that is the way that Inclusifyers support diversity. And that is why diversity, alone, is just not going to cut it.

So how can you ensure that your diversity is accompanied by

inclusion? Larry Kramer, the president of the William and Flora Hewlett Foundation, summed it up for me. He said that when he had taken over as president, he had made three decisions: "First, rather than spend a lot of time trying to shoehorn different matters into conceptual boxes like 'diversity,' 'equity,' or 'inclusion,' as if these are distinct categories to be separately delineated and characterized, we see them as words meant to capture different facets of an interrelated set of concerns that may touch anything and everything we do. Second, I'm not going to create a diversity office. It's part of the culture and strategy. Third, we're all responsible; each of us has to figure out what we can do."

INCLUSIFYING ACTION: **Aim for inclusion.**

One thing I enjoyed about my conversation with Kramer was how broadly he saw inclusion. If you are going to make it everyone's job, make it relevant to everyone. He said, "When we speak of diversity and inclusion, we mean the whole range of attitudes, outlooks, and perceptions that matter to the people who work with us—whether coming from familiar sources of personal identity, like race, gender, or religion; from less common sources that are particular to our institution, like a place in the foundation's hierarchy; or from sources that are idiosyncratic and individual in nature."

Rather than just saying "Don't let men speak over women," try encouraging people to use respectful communication.

One of the inclusion gaps that was considered at the Hewlett Foundation was the inclusion of people at different levels in the hierarchy. That made diversity and inclusion everyone's responsibility, and everyone was rewarded. The foundation's "Illustrative Practices" include the following:

- When hiring and recruiting staff, looking for candidates from a broad pool of qualified applicants with different backgrounds and experiences
- Paying attention to diversity when setting up search committees
- Striving to build a diverse staff and board by searching for candidates outside traditional and familiar networks
- Incorporating questions about the inclusion of diverse voices and perspectives in the OFP [Office of Fair Practices] guidance for strategy development and implementation
- Supporting sector efforts to increase diversity, equity, and inclusion
- Providing organizational effectiveness grants to help grantees with their own efforts to enhance the diversity, equity, and inclusiveness of their organizations
- Encouraging internal conversations in which varying viewpoints can be expressed
- Making training in cultural competency and in having difficult conversations available to all staff
- Collecting data about the diversity of our grantee pool and pursuing measures to combat the role of implicit and structural biases in our grantee selection
- Ensuring that we have considered the role of diversity, equity, and inclusion in the development of our grant making strategies[10]

The point is, once you achieve diversity, you are not done. Diversity requires inclusion. But think about it: according to a study by Deloitte, if you could boost the number of employees who feel included by only 10 percent, you would increase work attendance by one day per year *per employee*.[11] But just saying your company is inclusive is not enough; according to Deloitte, more than 80 percent of companies promote themselves as being highly inclusive, but only 11 percent really are.[12]

Most often, the problem is that although organizations give lip service to inclusive values, they're unwilling to make the structural revisions needed to actually create change, whether out of fear of threatening the majority, because it's too hard, or because they can't see what those changes should look like.

Chapter 15

LEADERSHIP STRATEGIES FOR OPTIMISTS

I have always been committed to diversity. When I came to Medtronic, it was always there, but just not at the level that I'm pushing it. It's become a little more visible. Perhaps the difference that I made is to bring this up to the CEO level and increase accountability around it. We are a good culture, we are a supportive culture, and we want to ensure that we are also an inclusive culture.

—OMAR ISHRAK, CEO, MEDTRONIC (INCLUSIFYER)

Most of the Inclusifyers I interviewed told me that at one time in their career they had been Optimists. They knew how important belonging is to an organization's success. They even recognized the importance of eliciting employees' uniqueness to improve decision-making and engagement. The only thing they were missing was the intentionality to make it happen.

The Optimist archetype became especially clear to me when I met the CEO of the Wikimedia Foundation, Katherine Maher, who told me the story of her journey from Optimist to Inclusifyer. She and I were both speaking at a conference at Yale, and I was so intrigued by how she described her Inclusifyer journey that I had to connect with her again for an interview.

"I was not terribly well informed about diversity and inclusion at all," she told me. "It is not that I didn't believe diversity was important, but I had a limited view. I would have said, 'I'm totally color blind.' I was an 'Oh, it'll happen with time' sort of person a few years ago. But the more I started learning about it, the more I was like 'Wow. No, it won't.'"

Just as with Benioff's realization at Salesforce, one of the pivotal moments for Maher was seeing a significant pay disparity between men and women at Wikipedia. From there, she became insatiably curious to learn more about diversity and inclusion. As a result of her investigation, she started to see the inequities among Wikipedia's staff and even in Wikipedia more broadly.

Then she came to the realization that optimism is not going to change society. Her words were poignant and eloquent: "The reality is that the 'It will fix itself over time' mentality doesn't work if every generation and every subsequent leader says 'It will fix itself over time.' Things only start getting better when you actually start doing the work. The position of saying there is no deadline on this or that things will right themselves in the world is an ahistorical way of looking at the way that advances have been made in terms of equity and representation. It has always required people to do the work. It has always required people to stand up and make it a priority. It has always required people to sacrifice other priorities in order to place their attention on making progress in this space or any area of equity and equal rights."

As she explained, the mission of Wikipedia is to serve every single human being on the planet, but she came to realize that it could not do that if its primary contributors continued to be American white men. She noted that even in 2016, only 14 percent of biographies on the entire website were about women. "So for us, diversity is not just something that is the right thing to do. It is the only way that we are going to actually get close to achieving the mission that we have for ourselves, and it is something that starts with ensuring a diversity of perspectives in our employees so that we can serve an increasingly diverse user community in order to have a product that is more inclusive than the product that we currently have today, which in turn makes it more accessible to more people."

And her commitment shows. Among new hires in the United States during the 2017–18 fiscal year, 65 percent were women and 43 percent were black/African American, Hispanic/Latino, or Asian. She achieved those numbers by updating the company's hiring practices, rethinking board recruitment, and starting employee resource groups.

She summed up her transition from Optimist to Inclusifyer by saying, "If you are not uncomfortable, you are probably not pushing yourself hard enough. It's a constant, active process of building a more diverse workforce, but then building the inclusive spaces that people need in order to continue to be successful, to feel satisfied, engaged, rewarded."

Following Maher's advice, the only thing impeding an Optimist from becoming an Inclusifyer is lack of decisive action. You need to mirror the support you feel in your heart with the support you exhibit in your actions. This is *Flying in Front of the Radar*. At the same time, you can use your natural positivity and increase your employees' motivation by making uniqueness and belonging (or Inclusifying) a more fun experience for everyone.

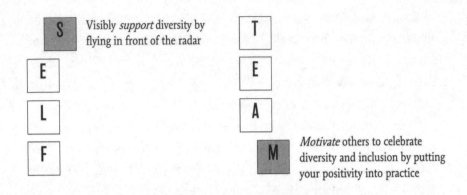

S   Visibly *support* diversity by flying in front of the radar

E

L

F

T

E

A

M   *Motivate* others to celebrate diversity and inclusion by putting your positivity into practice

FLY IN FRONT OF THE RADAR (SUPPORT)

One of the first steps Optimists can take to move into becoming Inclusifyers is to be more public with their commitment to championing uniqueness and belonging.

Customers today want to spend their money at companies that share their values. In fact, a survey by Sprout Social showed that 66 percent of respondents believed that it is important for brands to take a stand on social and political issues.[1] In most cases, that means standing up for inclusion.

Many of today's Inclusifying CEOs are activists at heart. PayPal's Dan Schulman told me that he had gained his commitment for activism from his mother, who had marched with Martin Luther King Jr., in the South. That was why Schulman canceled plans to open a new global operations center in Charlotte, North Carolina, in response to the state's Public Facilities Privacy & Security Act, which some feared would allow discrimination against the LGBTQ community. His stance meant the loss of four hundred jobs to the state. "The law perpetuates discrimination and violates the values that are at the core of PayPal's culture," he said in a statement released by PayPal back in 2016. The next year,

Schulman blocked PayPal's services to more than three dozen hate groups and white supremacist groups after some of them initiated a spate of deadly violence in Charlottesville. Dan saw the US government shutdown in early 2019 as a moment where the private sector needed to step up. He initiated the idea for PayPal to offer $500 in interest-free cash advances to furloughed US government workers, providing up to $25 million in interest-free loans. And more recently, following a survey of its global customer operations function, PayPal introduced a financial wellness program for its employees to increase wages, lower the cost of—yet enhance—benefits, make every employee a shareholder of PayPal, and provide financial planning and education tools.

I saw similar levels of activism among many of the CEOs I interviewed: John Rogers Jr., a co-CEO of Ariel Investments; Bernard Tyson, the late CEO of Kaiser Permanente; Marc Benioff of Salesforce; Katherine Maher of the Wikipedia Foundation. Leaders who have really bought into the importance of diversity will often adopt it as part of their worldview, and the next thing you know, they find themselves fighting for Dreamers over immigration laws or equal rights for LGBTQ or pay equality.

Even a new CEO can have a huge Inclusifying effect. When Jim Powers took over as CEO of the professional services firm Crowe LLP, he publicly stated that diversity and inclusion was a top strategic priority. Several years later, he consistently communicates and reinforces diversity with distinct alignment to the firm's long-standing core values and with a clear focus on both the business and moral case. I saw his passion, firsthand, when I spoke at their all-partners meeting back in 2018. He explained that his goal was to ensure the efforts become so much a part of the fabric of the firm, with observable impact, that they stand the test of time.

All of the employees I interviewed at Crowe agreed that Powers' stance on diversity was sending a clear message and that message was trickling down to affect other managers' behavior. Ray Calvey, audit partner at Crowe, told me, "Part of what the CEO has said is that he wants people to be active advocates for diversity and inclusion. Some people say, 'Well, I'm not *against* it.' That's great you're not *against* it, but Jim challenges us to ask, 'What am I doing to *promote* it?' Those are two very different things. For example, on my team, I set a goal that we were going to increase our overall diversity around race and gender over a three-year period. So, we measured ourselves on it: Are we getting more diverse, or are we not?

"We then had to say, 'Well, how do we increase the pipeline of people who are diverse who could come in and be the best candidate?' I can't hire the best diverse candidate if I never see any. And what you often will hear is, 'Well, there aren't any.' Well, we all know that's not accurate. There are people. It's just we're not going to the right places to find them. Part of it is really challenging yourself. Where am I sourcing candidates? How am I putting them through the filter? How do you actually rate people objectively? Because we all make judgments about people no matter who we are, either by their name or what they look like."

So, what is Crowe doing to create change? According to Chief People Officer Julie Wood, the firm set goals for increasing diversity in the candidate pipeline, as well as with promotions within the firm with a focus on ensuring those being hired and promoted reflect the available pool of talent. Karen Thompson, D&I Leader at Crowe, says the firm is also experimenting with technology solutions intended to remove bias in the recruitment process and new approaches to engage with underrepresented groups to better understand their experiences so that real change can be created to make things better. These steps combined with the firm's affinity groups, grassroots activities across the firm's geographic footprint, and leveraging diversity champions are at the core of creating real and lasting change.

Increase Goals and Accountability

But Optimists cannot just pay lip service to their commitments; they need to take an approach like Crowe and have accountability around those goals. Goal-setting theory—the idea that you are able to achieve greater results if you set specific, measurable, agreed-upon, realistic, time-based (SMART) goals—has proved its benefits in a variety of settings.[2] Organizations around the world use it, and individuals use it to create personal improvement goals (learn a language, get fit, stop smoking).

Even though diversity initiatives have profound impact on bottom-line outcomes for organizations, many people feel uncomfortable with setting diversity goals. But the fact is, a meta-analysis (a study summarizing previously done studies) showed that setting goals was the number one most effective diversity intervention. And lots of companies have followed suit.

Many of the CEOs I spoke with for this book used goal setting. Some companies, such as Gap Inc. and Salesforce, set pay equity goals. Others, such as Medtronic and Starbucks, set numeric goals for increasing diversity in their leadership. When I spoke at Accenture's International Women's Day celebration, I learned that the consulting giant had set a goal of 50 percent gender balance in its organization worldwide by 2025. It is currently at 40 percent. It also has set a goal of having 25 percent female managing directors.

Clearly, to set goals you have to know what your current numbers look like. Then you need to create a SMART goal. Then you need to come up with an action plan for how you will achieve that

goal. Lather, rinse, and repeat to ensure that you are making progress toward the goal.

As an example, Bob Wendelgass, the CEO of Clean Water Action, set goals for diversity. The association started by looking at
its diversity numbers, which was easy because it reports them to
Green 2.0 during its annual diversity survey. Then it committed to
having 30 percent of its board and 40 percent of its staff be people
of color. Wendelgass added diversity and inclusion to performance
evaluations, explaining, "I wanted to send the message that this
is not a nice-to-have or even a choice. This is something that the
organization is committed to, and it is part of your job. It is part
of every person's job, so it is part of the performance evaluation."

Of course, setting goals is pretty meaningless without accountability, and one of the things that really differentiates Inclusifyers
from Optimists is their emphasis on accountability. Just as important as having goals is having accountability around those
goals. Most people aren't evil; they rely on stereotypes because it
is easy to do so. So people need a compelling reason to interrupt
stereotypes. Accountability is one of those reasons.

A great longitudinal field study surveyed nine thousand employees to examine the effects of accountability and transparency
in pay decisions.[3] The researchers looked at the pay gap before
and after management introduced accountability and transparency
into the company's performance reward system. Before the intervention, there was a gap in the distribution of performance-based
rewards such that white men received more rewards than did
women, minorities, and non-US-born employees who *had the same
scores on their performance evaluations* and worked in the same job
with the same manager! However, the gap was reduced after the
organization increased transparency and accountability

One company I consulted for took accountability to the next

level. In a phenomenon called the decoy effect, individuals are naturally attracted to the two most similar options of three and, to limit cognitive effort, will focus their efforts on choosing between the two similar options and ignore the third, different option. Based on my research on finalist slates (when finalist slates have only one non-white man, a white man is disproportionately likely to be hired),[4] it first required that every finalist slate have at least two women, POC, WOC, and/or LGBTQ (or one woman and one POC).

Second, to increase accountability, the chief diversity officer required that every time a white male was hired into the company, the hiring manager would have to clarify why a woman or POC had not been hired. This might sound extreme, but he explained that for decades he had been forced to explain why and justify every woman or POC he had hired because white men had been the status quo. Hiring a woman or POC had always represented a perceived risk, so he had always had to make the case for them. What if he flipped the script and required hiring managers to justify the hiring of a white man? He found that it caused people to put a lot more thought into their hiring decisions rather than just opting for the easy choice.

But goal setting is not limited to employees; organizations should set goals for supplier diversity as well. Dawn Chase, the head of diversity and inclusion at the NAACP, explained to me how important supplier diversity is to equality and suggests that even in cases where organizations cannot find black-owned suppliers, they should look for suppliers who use black-owned subcontractors. PepsiCo has been committed to supplier diversity since 1982, and setting goals is at the heart of that effort.[5] Consistent with Dawn Chase's suggestion, they direct their nondiverse suppliers to use minority-owned subcontractors and require them to report the number of subcontractor dollars that are spent on minority-owned subcontractors.

PUT POSITIVITY INTO PRACTICE (MOTIVATE)

The second lesson, *Put Positivity into Practice*, capitalizes on Optimists' already positive attitude and translates it into action: motivating team members by celebrating diversity. The reality is that most people prefer diversity over homogeneity. People who work in more diverse and inclusive environments are more engaged, committed, collaborative, and satisfied with their jobs. According to Deloitte and the Billie Jean King Leadership Initiative, millennials expect greater levels of diversity in their workforce.[6] This is even more true for Gen Z, which includes those born between 1995 and 2015. As the most diverse generation to date, Gen Zers demand diversity and equality at work.[7]

I have noticed that television shows are becoming more diverse, which makes me more likely to watch them. Think of Shonda Rhimes's amazing casts on shows such as *Grey's Anatomy*, which, after its 332nd episode in February 2019, became television's longest-running prime-time medical drama,[8] and the stereotype-busting, record-breaking *Scandal*, at the time of its launch in 2012 the first network drama to star a black woman in forty years.[9] So I was not terribly surprised when I started seeing research studies showing that most people prefer more diverse casts—a preference that translates into bottom-line outcomes.

In a study conducted at UCLA, researchers analyzed the two hundred highest-grossing films in 2016—think *Captain America: Civil War* and *Suicide Squad*. Movies in which 21 to 30 percent of the cast were minorities grossed a median global box office revenue of $179.2 million. In contrast, films with less than 10 percent minority actors grossed a median of less than $40 million worldwide.[10] In another study, researchers found that diverse movies—specifically those with more than one black actor—outperformed those with one or zero black actors.[11] To rule out alternative explanations (such as the higher-performing movies having larger casts or bigger budgets), they replicated their findings used a controlled laboratory experiment and found the same effect. As the US population becomes more diverse, people feel more comfortable in diverse workspaces.

So why not celebrate diversity? Many Inclusifyers I spoke with told me that they created rites and rituals that celebrate uniqueness and belonging so that doing so doesn't feel like a chore. For example, the food service and facilities management company Sodexo has a Champions of Diversity Program in which individuals and teams can be recognized for a wide variety of actions that support diversity and inclusion, from large-scale programs such as creating employee resource groups to small acts such as coaching and mentoring. Nominations are made online, and the winners receive awards and a commendation letter from the company's global diversity officer, Rohini Anand. The winners also get to have a team-building event and are recognized in company media. Even just sharing stories of Inclusifyed success is a great way to reinforce the culture.

American Family Insurance kicks off LGBTQ Pride Month with a flag-raising ceremony at its national headquarters and has a "Wear Your Pride" week when it encourages employees to wear a specific color each day. Company employees have also participated in Pride parades in Denver, Colorado; St. Joseph, Missouri; and Eden Prairie, Minnesota.

Squarespace, which has been voted the best place to work in

New York for two years by *Crain's New York Business*, promotes belonging by focusing on a flat, open, creative culture. To help employees feel that their voices are heard and listened to, the CEO has office hours that anyone can attend. The company also hosts great events, such as a monthly new-hire social. The social is hosted in the office café/bar area, and food, drinks, and games are provided. There is a slideshow with every new hire's photo, his or her team, and a fun fact about him or her to help get the conversation started. There is a "question of the month," such as "What's your favorite TV show theme song?" to help employees get to know one another. The company also has an annual summer party, on-site arts and crafts, life-size checkers, minigolf, and food from local vendors.

The consulting company Team Building Hero suggests holding events such as scavenger hunts, escape rooms, bowling, cupcake competitions, and book swaps (share *Inclusify* with someone!) to help people get to know one another.

Many companies, such as Adobe and REI, strive to create more fun at work, and this can have positive effects. For example, one study showed that having more fun at work improved employees' quality of life and even resulted in their sleeping better. In contrast, being exposed to workplace incivility—rude or hostile interactions at work—can result in a worse quality of life, lower workplace performance, decreased collaboration, and increased turnover. Fun work environments are just better and, not surprisingly, more conducive to creativity and diversity.

Inclusifyed Workplace Activities
- Celebrate Inclusifyed accomplishments.
- Name an "Inclusifyer of the Month."
- Hold scavenger hunts.

- Visit an escape room.
- Go bowling.
- Hold a cupcake-baking competition.
- Hold a book swap.
- Hold surprise birthday parties, baby showers, etc.
- Celebrate Pride Week and other cultural events.
- Hold new-hire socials.
- Ask a question of the month to encourage communication.
- Hold a summer party.
- Do on-site arts and crafts.
- Make a life-size checkerboard.
- Play minigolf.
- Eat lunch or dinner together.
- Watch sporting events together.

Activities such as these can help infuse an Inclusifyed culture into the fabric of an organization. I feel the best example of this has been Starbucks's culture and brand centered on the human experience. The company has 90 million customers a week in 26,000 stores around the world, and it works to help employees and customers feel connected. When Starbucks founder and long-time CEO Howard Schultz retired in 2017, I became curious about whether the new CEO, Kevin Johnson, would uphold those values.

I requested an interview with Johnson within his first week as CEO for an article I was writing for the *Harvard Business Review*. Honestly, I was a little surprised that he agreed to talk with me; he was pretty busy running Starbucks and all. But he said that the issue of creating more diverse and inclusive workplaces is so important to him and to Starbucks that he had to take the time.

Luckily, he is every bit the Inclusifyer that Schultz is, and he explained how focusing on an Inclusifyed culture is central to Starbucks's success. Starbucks' culture really revolves around creating a culture of compassion and empathy where people can connect. This starts with how it aspires to treat its customers and extends to how employees treat one another.

Importantly, Johnson does not optimistically hope that the company culture will continue but instead works every day to make it happen, in the process making real strides in terms of diversity on his executive team and board.

Chapter 16

MY INCLUSIFY JOURNEY

It's a journey to really understand the many ways that race and gender affect our world. There's always deeper and deeper levels of discovery and understanding around diversity and inclusion.
—LOIS DEBACKER, MANAGING DIRECTOR, KRESGE FOUNDATION
(INCLUSIFYER)

Just like all of the other leaders out there, I was not born an Inclusifyer. I have suffered from several of the follies at different points in my life, and sometimes I still demonstrate a little sprinkle and a dash of a couple of them. You might feel the same. Maybe you are not 100 percent Meritocracy Manager but more like 40 percent Meritocracy Manager, 40 percent Culture Crusader, and 20 percent Inclusifyer. I think that is normal. It is a journey, and this is my mine.

YOUNG STEFANIE

For a little context, I will tell you about my background. I grew up with my mom (my parents were divorced) in Los Angeles. We lived pretty close to East LA, which has been a traditionally Hispanic area but also includes a large Asian population. My high school was something like 48 percent Hispanic, 48 percent Asian, and 4 percent other. My mom is Mexican, my dad was Caucasian. I speak Spanish (poorly) and love being Latino.

If I had to think of a single word to describe my childhood, the word that stands out is *poor*. Lots of people will tell me that they grew up poor and then that their mom was a doctor. That's not the kind of poor I am talking about. Neither of my parents went to college. At different times in my life we were on welfare and food stamps. We were free-turkey-for-Thanksgiving kind of poor. My mom would disagree because she always felt blessed. Maybe so, but we were *at least* financially poor.

I don't think it would be too much of a stretch to say that I was always an odd kid. I have always been awkwardly tall, standing 5 feet, 10½ inches since age fourteen. I am not particularly athletic, although I played lots of sports in high school. In fact, I think I tried a little bit of everything in high school in the hope of finding some type of magic formula to get into college. I heard that colleges like athletes, students who hold down jobs, or students with lots of AP credits. I wasn't really sure which was correct, so I just tried to do it all. I was in drama, yearbook, newspaper, social clubs, and student council.

In my mind, I really never fit in, but when I went to my twenty-year high school reunion, I was astonished to learn that other people seemed to think I had fit in great. "You were class president!" a friend said ironically. "How could it be that you did not fit in?" I'm actually pretty sure that I was vice president, but that's beside the point.

I guess she must have been right; I seemed to fit in. But the thing is, I never felt that I *belonged*. And now, looking back, I see that the reason was that I was never myself. I was an extreme chameleon. In psychology, we call this self-monitoring, which is the ability to read social situations and *fit in* no matter what. But when you are always acting to fit in, it is easy to lose your sense of who you are. And really, we don't need to fit in, we just need to find a way to fit together.

Despite the disadvantages I faced as a kid, I was able to be accepted by the best colleges in the United States. Though I thought I deserved those admissions (after all, I had followed a formula), my admission to those schools was questioned by others. I remember one of my friends from high school telling me outright that I had been admitted to UC Berkeley only because of my race. At the time, the state of California had just passed Proposition 209, which made it illegal for public universities to consider race in the admission process. As the law went through, the percentage of Latino students admitted to the UC system actually decreased from 15.1 percent to 13.4 percent.

Wanting to prove myself caused me to experience a little stereotype threat (I was afraid I would fail and confirm the stereotype that Mexican kids are less than in some way). I also started to embrace the concept of meritocracy. In some ways I felt as though if I could succeed, isn't that proof that the world is a meritocracy?

COLLEGE DAZE

I carried some stereotype threat and meritocratic ideals into college but I also started to see the importance of being myself rather than just trying to fit in. I think finding one's identity is part of anyone's college experience, and I started trying to balance uniqueness and belonging during my first year of school. I had just arrived on one of the most beautiful college campuses in the United States, Claremont McKenna College. It was known to be a party school, and it was filled with smart, beautiful people who looked as though they had just stepped out of a reality TV show. There were parties every night of orientation week, and despite my tendency toward introversion, I managed to get out to all of them with my new roommates and floor mates.

But as Friday rolled around, I knew there was going to be a problem. Friday was the most important night of the week for my eighteen-year-old self: it was when a new episode of *The X-Files* would air on Fox. But there was also a toga party happening that night. When it came down to choosing between the two, the winner was clear: true believer of the paranormal Mulder and his skeptical partner, Scully, of course. I figured no one would care if I didn't go to the party, and if they did, they were probably not my kind of people, anyway.

But I was wrong; people cared. In a time when everyone was looking for ways to place themselves in the in-group, gossiping about the nerd in their midst was perfect fodder for conversation. Because of my taste for toxic soda and dark TV shows, people thought I was weird, and one way to try to fit in is by pushing other people out. The next morning at breakfast I overheard another student say, "Did you hear about the girl from Faucet [my dorm] who ditched the party last night to watch TV?" From that day on, I was relentlessly mocked for passing up an opportunity to wear a sheet and drink cheap beer in favor of lying on a sheet and drinking Mountain Dew in front of the *The X-Files*.

I was trying to tell people about me—trying to be my unique

self. I was the girl whose high school yearbook quote was: "The truth is out there." A person who would never attend concerts because they are too crowded, but found the strength to go to an *X-Files* convention. Someone who secretly stalked the male costar of the show, David Duchovny, who, interestingly, almost took a job at Claremont McKenna College before landing his big role (that was a coincidence, I assure you, and not the reason I chose to go to school there).

So, just like many other college students, even though I wanted to belong, I did not want to belong if I could not be me. Let's be honest, I could have pretended that I was sick or gone to the party and missed that one episode of *The X-Files* if I had really wanted to fit in. But I didn't want just to fit in; I wanted to fit in as myself.

I found my identity in other ways as well, doing research on leadership all four years of college, including a college senior thesis. I attended academic conferences as a college student and continued my quest for a PhD, still believing that the world was a meritocracy and I would get into grad school.

PHD SCHOOL

After college I went straight into a PhD program at Rice University, where I learned much more about statistics and how to conduct research on leadership (the topic of my master's thesis and dissertation). But I also started to learn that the world was not so meritocratic after all. As the instructor or teaching assistant for different classes, I realized that the playing field is not level. I saw that some students have lower GPAs because they have to work to pay for school. But that does not make them less smart, it just means that they are less wealthy. I realized that many talented students are lost because of money, family responsibilities, and bias in higher education.

When I was a student working my way through college, I was too wrapped up in my ego to see the inequality. I did not want to admit that I had to work harder than other people just to pay for books. In fact, I did not want anyone to know that I had to work. But now, when it was not about me, I could clearly see that inequities exist within the ivory tower.

To be fair, I still engaged in a lot of behaviors that upheld the patriarchy, as I like to say. I applied to work only with male PhD advisers because I figured they would have more connections and credibility to help get me a job. I never framed my research around diversity because I thought that would make people see me as less competent or serious. Instead, I studied leadership—a nice masculine topic. I tried not to annoy people by talking about inequality.

But I started to see how systems were imperfect and often impeded the success of women and people of color. My graduate cohort was actually pretty diverse, including one black woman, one Hispanic woman (that's me), one Hispanic man, and three white women. But the rest of academia did not look so diverse. I remember one of my first job interviews at a conference. The interview took place in a hotel room—not a conference room, a room with an actual bed in it. When I walked in, feeling pretty sketched out, I met three white men who each had a copy of my résumé in front of him. They gave one another strange looks, and it was so awkward that I finally interjected, "Is something wrong?" One of the trio responded with a Southern drawl, "We just thought that you would be *older*."

I had finished my PhD at twenty-five, and at that point, I was probably twenty-six. So they had me there. I was certainly young, and I had already heard the message that business schools don't like to hire young female faculty because the MBA students will "eat them alive" and give them poor teaching evaluations. In fact, there is extensive evidence of unfair bias against women in teaching evaluations, but that does not seem to be a very fair way to hire people.[1]

Trying to think of a funny quip with which to respond to "We thought that you would be older," I finally replied, "I will be." Long pause for effect. "Tomorrow, and the day after that and the day after that. Let's be honest, gentlemen, this train is only heading one direction." Silence. I smiled to try to show them I was joking. "Thank you, that will be all," they said, indicating that the interview was over.

PROFESSORHOOD

But of course, I did get a job at some point, and my teaching evaluations were fine. And I did get older, as expected. The main surprise that I faced was that nearly all of my studies on leadership revealed race and gender disparities. Seeing bias firsthand like this—in research, not just in anecdotes—angered me, and I started moving more toward being a Shepherd. I started trying to stand out and stand up for diversity and inclusion and got into quite a few arguments along the way. When you believe that someone is not supporting equality, it can be infuriating.

No workplace is perfect, and mine has definitely had ups and downs when it comes to diversity. But the ups have outweighed the downs because my department has been open to the idea of changing workplace practices to reduce bias. We did an anonymized job search that yielded two new female professors, tripling the number of women in my department (I used to be a solo). But then I overheard a colleague tell one of the women that we had hired her because she was a woman. "We really wanted to hire a woman," he said. Was that supposed to be a compliment? I quickly explained to both of them that we had done an anonymized search so we had not known she was a woman until we had invited her out to interview, but I am not sure that soothed the sting she must have felt.

The school has had its fair share of challenges when it comes to diversity, but we have also had triumphs championed by our dean, Sharon Matusik. She has launched several initiatives to recruit and retain a more diverse student body. In moving toward that goal, the stats on our new students (SATs, GPAs) also went up, as did our placement as number twenty in the ranking of best business schools in the country for undergraduate students. There are now five woman deans in our school, up from zero just a few years ago. And importantly, the dean has always been very transparent with her processes so that no one can accuse her of bias. I have been able to create a new course called Women in Business for undergraduate students and an MBA course on inclusive leadership. In many ways, I see Leeds as one of the leaders in creating an inclusive undergraduate business curriculum.

MOMHOOD AND LIFE

Just like any working mom, I experience the challenges of balancing work and family. I have seen how valuable workplace flexibility can be for parents. It is shocking how many elementary school events are scheduled in the middle of the day. I do my best to attend what I can, but I miss a lot, too. I love my work, so I try to convince myself that I am making the world a better place for my kids and setting a good example of gender equality by being a working mom. Of course, there are always pangs of mom guilt and moments of regrets when I think I have missed out on something the kids are doing. I travel a ton to deliver presentations at conferences, at different companies, and to many corporate boards. On those trips I am away from my family a lot. More recently, I have started to take the kids with me as I travel around, often accompanied by my mom, who can help watch the kiddos while I am working.

I also face the extraordinary challenge of raising culturally intelligent kids while living in a city that is 90 percent white. I was sitting at a delightful dinner with Mellody Hobson, co-CEO of Ariel Investments, when she asked what others at the table were doing for diversity and inclusion. Having learned about the folly of being an Optimist, I am very aware of the importance of taking action on diversity, rather than just paying it lip service. And I do a lot to mentor women, POC, WOC, students with disabilities, LGBTQ students, and first-generation college students. I give money. I give time. I really try to create change. But then she asked, "Can you can really create change when you live in a totally white community?" Slam. I had never thought about the fact that I had chosen to live in a place that so clearly lacks diversity, and coming from an Inclusifyer like her, the words had a lot of weight.

I mean, I did not move to Boulder because it lacked diversity. I just wanted to be walking or biking distance from my office. And there are really good schools and low crime—and wow! I am in many ways failing to uphold the values I espouse. Immediately, I went home and told my husband that we had to move back to California (we are both from Los Angeles), we needed to spend our sabbaticals in Mexico, or we needed to at least move our kids to a more diverse school. We have not done any of those things to date, and I am open to suggestions for change. But it does feel quite hypocritical not to live in a diverse community when I believe so strongly in diversity. So there is always progress to be made. I am in no way the paragon of diversity perfection. But I am trying every day to make changes on my own Inclusify journey.

SUMMING UP

Whether you're an Optimist, a Shepherd, or a little bit of everything including Inclusifyer, the lessons in this book are designed to help you enhance uniqueness and belonging in your organization. Feel free to use something from the Team Player chapter that resonated with you, even if you are a Meritocracy Manager. They all work. I encourage you to choose one or two things to try out at work or any of these topics to start a conversation in your office. That will already put you a step ahead by increasing your empathy.

You read this book for a reason. You know that leaders grow and change all of the time. And if you didn't know before that there is a dramatic need for more inclusive workplace practices, you do now. I hope that you enjoy your Inclusifyer journey. Remember: it should be fun, it will be challenging, you will make mistakes, you will recover, and in the end you will emerge as a better, stronger leader.

There are many places you can start on your journey. Of course, you can pull the lessons from the chapter that most resonated with you (you can also take the Inclusify assessment at InclusifyBook .com), or you can just pick your favorite from the book. In reality, doing anything is better than doing nothing. And remember, as you go on the Inclusify journey, you need to first make your unconscious biases conscious and then start engaging in intentional actions to Inclusify. Then do it all over again.

If I had to recommend one place to start, it would be empathy. Start talking to people so that you can better understand their perspectives. Try mentoring people who are different from you—in a mentoring circle or one on one. Create an amplification network in your office to open conversations up to other people. Ask them about the cultural practices that are not inclusive, and think about how you can make swaps. The next time you call a meeting, try to design for dissension and notice how much more effective it feels. Those are all great places to start.

You may notice that some of the lessons are easy for you to do alone, while others require a bit more structural change, and therefore you might need to get a few more people on board to help you with your efforts. The lessons that require only your individual effort can be a great place to start, because you can always build on the simple behavior by addressing the topic with your team. For example, you might start with empathy by *Walking in Their Shoes* (talking to people in your office to learn more about their perspectives). But you can make that action more concrete by

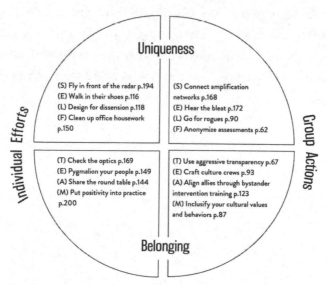

trying to *Hear the Bleat* (telling your team to feel free to come to you in a group if they feel they have experienced unfair treatment). When you start to combine those individual efforts with more structural changes, that's when the real magic happens.

If you are a human resources or diversity leader, I hope you found the diversity and inclusion practices in the book to be useful. Try recruiting from diverse networks, ensuring diverse slates, using anonymizing assessments in your initial screening, and always following the D-C-B-A (Define Criteria Before Assessing) principle in selection. Go for rogues, and try to capture the jets. Beyond selection, consider changes such as cleaning up office housework, creating bystander intervention training, and creating culture crews. Find ways to celebrate your diversity and inclusion successes.

If you are the CEO, president, or executive director of your organization, start change from the top. Fly in front of the radar so everyone knows where you stand on diversity and inclusion. Incorporate uniqueness and belonging into the mission, vision, and values of your organization. Set SMART goals, and be aggressively transparent while always checking the optics and ensuring that you share the table with the white men in your organization. Do something. Do anything. But do it today and keep moving forward on your Inclusifyer journey.

ACKNOWLEDGMENTS

Thank you to: My Swiet Piet for supporting my dream of writing this book. My children, who are the reasons that I know we can create a better future. My mamoo, who keeps me grounded, and my brother, whom I lost too young but who always stood up for me. My friends who listened to me talk about this for the last year: Elli, Nathalie, Courtney, Anisha, Sherice, and Jenny. My agent, Michael Palgon, and Tasha Eurich for introducing us. The staff at HarperCollins, who were so invaluable in this process. My list of Inclusifying mentors: Bob Dipboye, Mikki Hebl, Ron Riggio, and Susan Murphy. All of the CEOs and other leaders who gave their time to talk to a random business professor, but most of all Marc Benioff, Ralph de Chabert, Billie Jean King, and John Rogers, who opened many doors for me. All of my students, who are smarter and better than I could ever be but inspire me to continue trying to solve the most important questions that businesses face. All of the women, POC, WOC, LGBTQ, and persons with disabilities who fought for equality when it seemed as though it would never happen. Thank you all.

NOTES

Introduction

1. Sonali K. Shah, Rajshree Agarwal, and Raj Echambadi, "Jewels in the Crown: Exploring the Motivations and Team Building Processes of Employee Entrepreneurs," *Strategic Management Journal* 40, no. 9 (2019): 1417–52.

2. Paul A. Gompers and Sophie Q. Wang, "Diversity in Innovation," Working Paper no. 23082, National Bureau of Economic Research, January 2017, https://www.nber.org/papers/w23082.pdf.

3. Susan Sorenson, "How Employee Engagement Drives Growth," Gallup, June 20, 2013, https://www.gallup.com/workplace/236927/employee-engagement-drives-growth.aspx.

4. Marilynn B. Brewer, "Optimal Distinctiveness Theory: Its History and Development," in *Handbook of Theories of Social Psychology*, vol. 2, ed. Paul A. M. Van Lange, Arie W. Kruglanski, and E. Tory Higgins (London: Sage, 2011), 81–98.

5. Lynn M. Shore, Amy E. Randel, Beth G. Chung, et al., "Inclusion and Diversity in Work Groups: A Review and Model for Future Research," *Journal of Management* 37, no. 4 (2011): 1262–89.

6. "When Women Thrive: An Evidence Based Approach to Diversity and Inclusion," Mercer, https://www.mercer.com/our-thinking/when-women-thrive.html.

Chapter 1: The Power of Uniqueness and Belonging

1. Geoff MacDonald and Mark R. Leary, "Why Does Social Exclusion Hurt? The Relationship Between Social and Physical Pain," *Psychological Bulletin* 131, no. 2 (2005): 202–23.

2. Kristen P. Jones, Chad I. Peddie, Veronica L. Gilrane, et al., "Not So Subtle: A Meta-Analytic Investigation of the Correlates of Subtle and Overt Discrimination," *Journal of Management* 42, no. 6 (2016): 1588–1613.

3. Blake E. Ashforth and Fred Mael, "Social Identity Theory and the Organization," *Academy of Management Review* 14, no. 1 (1989): 20–39.

4. Kimberlé Crenshaw, "Demarginalizing the Intersection of Race and Sex: A Black Feminist Critique of Antidiscrimination Doctrine, Feminist Theory and Antiracist Politics," *The University of Chicago Legal Forum* 1989, no. 1 (1989): article 8.

5. Alexis Nicole Smith, Maria Baskerville, Jamie J. Ladge, and Pamela Carlton, "Making the Invisible Visible: Paradoxical Effects of Intersectional Invisibility on the Career Experiences of Executive Black Women in the Workplace," *Academy of Management Journal* (in press). Ashleigh Shelby Rosette, Christy Zhou Koval, Anyi Ma, and Robert W. Livingston, "Race Matters for Women Leaders: Intersectional Effects on Agentic Deficiencies and Penalties," *The Leadership Quarterly* 27, no. 3 (2016): 429–45. Ashleigh Shelby Rosette and Robert W. Livingston, "Failure Is Not an Option for Black Women: Effects of Organizational Performance on Leaders with Single Versus Dual-Subordinate Identities," *Journal of Experimental Social Psychology* 48, no. 5 (2012): 1162–67.

6. Patricia Faison Hewlin, "Wearing the Cloak: Antecedents and Consequences of Creating Facades of Conformity," *Journal of Applied Psychology* 94, no. 3 (2009): 727–41.

7. Robin J. Ely and David A. Thomas, "Cultural Diversity at Work: The Effects of Diversity Perspectives on Work Group Processes and Outcomes," *Administrative Science Quarterly* 46, no. 2 (2001): 229–73.

8. Verónica Caridad Rabelo and Ramaswami Mahalingam, "'They Really Don't Want to See Us': How Cleaners Experience Invisible 'Dirty' Work," *Journal of Vocational Behavior* 113 (2019): 103–114.

9. Amber Burton, "Women of Color: Invisible, Excluded and Constantly 'On Guard,'" *Wall Street Journal*, December 9, 2019, https://www.wsj.com/articles/women-of-color-invisible-excluded-and-constantly-on-guard-11571112060. Isis H. Settles, NiCole T. Buchanan, and

Kristie Dotson, "Scrutinized but Not Recognized: (In)visibility and Hypervisibility Experiences of Faculty of Color," *Journal of Vocational Behavior* 113 (2019): 62–74. Kerrie G. Wilkins-Yel, Jacqueline Hyman, and Nelson O. O. Zounlome, "Linking Intersectional Invisibility and Hypervisibility to Experiences of Microaggressions Among Graduate Women of Color in STEM," *Journal of Vocational Behavior* 113 (2019): 51–61.

10. Anne-Marie Slaughter, Joan C. Williams, and Rachel Dempsey, *What Works for Women at Work: Four Patterns Working Women Need to Know* (New York: NYU Press, 2014).

11. Tsedal B. Neeley, "Language Matters: Status Loss and Achieved Status Distinctions in Global Organizations," *Organization Science* 24, no. 2 (2013): 476–97.

12. Danielle D. Dickens, Veronica Y. Womack, and Treshae Dimes, "Managing Hypervisibility: An Exploration of Theory and Research on Identity Shifting Strategies in the Workplace Among Black Women," *Journal of Vocational Behavior* 113 (2019): 153–63. Courtney L. McCluney and Verónica Caridad Rabelo, "Conditions of Visibility: An Intersectional Examination of Black Women's Belongingness and Distinctiveness at Work," *Journal of Vocational Behavior* 113 (2019): 143–52.

13. Kristen P. Jones and Eden B. King, "Managing Concealable Stigmas at Work: A Review and Multilevel Model," *Journal of Management* 40, no. 5 (2014): 1466–494.

14. Isaac E. Sabat, Alex P. Lindsey, Eden B. King, et al., "Stigma Expression Outcomes and Boundary Conditions: A Meta-Analysis," *Journal of Business and Psychology* (2019): 1–16. Anna M. Kallschmidt, and Asia A. Eaton, "Are Lower Social Class Origins Stigmatized at Work? A Qualitative Study of Social Class Concealment and Disclosure Among White Men Employees Who Experienced Upward Mobility," *Journal of Vocational Behavior* 113 (2019): 115–28.

15. McCluney and Rabelo, "Conditions of Visibility."

16. Marla Baskerville Watkins, Aneika Simmons, and Elizabeth Umphress, "It's Not Black and White: Toward a Contingency Perspective on the Consequences of Being a Token," *Academy of Management Perspectives* 33, no. 3 (2019): 334–65.

Chapter 2: The ABCs of Breaking Bias

1. Anthony G. Greenwald and Mahzarin R. Banaji, "Implicit Social Cognition: Attitudes, Self-Esteem, and Stereotypes," *Psychological Review* 102, no. 1 (1995): 4–27. Anthony G. Greenwald and Linda Hamilton Krieger, "Implicit Bias: Scientific Foundations," *California Law Review* 94, no. 4 (2006): 945–67. Anthony G. Greenwald, "New Look 3: Unconscious Cognition Reclaimed," *American Psychologist* 47, no. 6 (1992): 766.

2. Mahzarin R. Banaji and Anthony G. Greenwald, *Blindspot: Hidden Biases of Good People* (New York: Bantam, 2016).

3. Greenwald and Banaji, "Implicit Social Cognition: Attitudes, Self-Esteem, and Stereotypes."

4. Laura Mather, "Dear White Men: Five Pieces of Advice for 91 Percent of Fortune 500 CEOs," *HuffPost*, August 4, 2016, https://www.huffpost.com/entry/dear-white-men-seven-piec_b_7899084.

5. Claire Cain Miller, Kevin Quealy, and Margot Sanger-Katz, "The Top Jobs Where Women Are Outnumbered by Men Named John," *New York Times*, April 24, 2018, https://www.nytimes.com/interactive/2018/04/24/upshot/women-and-men-named-john.html.

6. Susan T. Fiske, Amy J. C. Cuddy, and Peter Glick, "Universal Dimensions of Social Cognition: Warmth and Competence," *Trends in Cognitive Sciences* 11, no. 2 (2007): 77–83.

7. Daniel M. Wegner, David J. Schneider, Samuel R. Carter III, and Teri L. White, "Paradoxical Effects of Thought Suppression," *Journal of Personality and Social Psychology* 53, no. 1 (1987): 5–13.

8. Juan M. Madera and Michelle R. Hebl, "Discrimination Against Facially Stigmatized Applicants in Interviews: An Eye-Tracking and Face-to-Face Investigation," *Journal of Applied Psychology* 97, no. 2 (2012): 317–30.

9. Daniel M. Wegner, "When the Antidote Is the Poison: Ironic Mental Control Processes," *Psychological Science* 8, no. 3 (1997): 148–50.

10. Jessica Nordell, "Is This How Discrimination Ends?," *The Atlantic*, May 7, 2017, https://www.theatlantic.com/science/archive/2017/05/unconscious-bias-training/525405/.

Chapter 3: Three Lessons to Put You on the Path to Inclusifying

1. Marc Benioff, *Trailblazer: The Power of Business as the Greatest Platform for Change* (New York: Currency, 2019).

2. Carolyn L. Hafer and Laurent Bègue, "Experimental Research on Just-World Theory: Problems, Developments, and Future Challenges," *Psychological Bulletin* 131, no. 1 (2005): 128–67.

3. Jamal Carnette, "Salesforce's 3-Year Growth Streak Is More Impressive Than It Appears," The Motley Fool, June 5, 2018, https://www.fool.com/investing/2018/06/05/salesforces-3-year-growth-streak-is-more-impressiv.aspx.

4. Dolly Chugh, *The Person You Mean to Be: How Good People Fight Bias* (New York: HarperCollins, 2018).

5. Angela Duckworth, *Grit: The Power of Passion and Perseverance* (New York: Scribner, 2016).

6. Christopher J. Bryan, Carol S. Dweck, Lee Ross, et al., "Political Mindset: Effects of Schema Priming on Liberal-Conservative Political Positions," *Journal of Experimental Social Psychology* 45, no. 4 (2009): 890–95.

7. Ashley Shelby Rosette and Christy Zhou Koval, "Framing Advantageous Inequity with a Focus on Others: A Catalyst for Equity Restoration," *Journal of Experimental Social Psychology* 76 (May 2018): 283–89.

8. "Economic Diversity and Student Outcomes at Yale University," *New York Times*, https://www.nytimes.com/interactive/projects/college-mobility/yale-university.

9. Joanna Pearlstein, "The Schools Where Apple, Google, and Facebook Get Their Recruits," WIRED, May 22, 2014, https://www.wired.com/2014/05/alumni-network-2/.

10. Rose McGowan, *Brave* (New York: HarperCollins, 2018).

11. Stefanie K. Johnson, Ksenia Keplinger, Jessica F. Kirk, and Liza Y. Barnes. "Has Sexual Harassment Declined at Work Since #Metoo," https://hbr .org/2019/07/has-sexual-harassment-at-work-decreased-since-metoo; Ksenia Keplinger, Stefanie K. Johnson, Jessica F. Kirk, and Liza Y. Barnes. "Women at Work: Changes in Sexual Harassment Between September 2016 and September 2018," *PloS ONE* 14, no. 7 (2019).

12. Sexual harassment backlash survey. Lean In, 2018, https://leanin .org/ sexual-harassment-backlash-survey-results; W. B. Johnson, D. G. Smith, "Men Shouldn't Refuse to Be Alone with Female Colleagues." *Harvard Business Review,* May 5, 2017, https://hbr .org/ 2017/ 05/men –shouldnt-refuse-to-be-alone-with-female-colleagues. C. Cain Miller, "Unintended Consequences of Sexual Harassment Scandals," *New York Times,* October 9, 2017, https://www.nytimes .com/2017/10/09 /upshot/as-sexual-harassment-scandals-spook-men-it-can-backfire -for-women.html.

13. Ronan Farrow, *Catch and Kill: Lies, Spies, and a Conspiracy to Protect Predators* (New York: Little, Brown, and Company, 2019).

14. Brandon N. Cline, Ralph A. Walkling, and Adam S. Yore, "The Consequences of Managerial Indiscretions: Sex, Lies, and Firm Value," *Journal of Financial Economics* 127, no. 2 (2018): 389–415.

Chapter 4: Meritocracy Manager

1. Devah Pager, Bart Bonikowski, and Bruce Western, "Discrimination in a Low-Wage Labor Market: A Field Experiment," *American Sociological Review* 74, no. 5 (2009): 777–99.

2. Shreyansh Bhatt, Manas Gaur, Beth Bullemer, et al., "Enhancing Crowd Wisdom Using Explainable Diversity Inferred from Social Media," in *2018 IEEE/WIC/ACM International Conference on Web Intelligence (WI)* (Santaigo, Chile: IEEE, 2018), 293–300.

3. Emilio J. Castilla and Stephen Benard, "The Paradox of Meritocracy in Organizations," *Administrative Science Quarterly* 55, no. 4 (2010): 543–676.

4. Marsha B. Jacobson and Walter Koch, "Women as Leaders: Performance

Evaluation as a Function of Method of Leader Selection," *Organizational Behavior and Human Performance* 20, no. 1 (1977): 149–57.

5. Madeline E. Heilman, Caryn J. Block, and Peter Stathatos, "The Affirmative Action Stigma of Incompetence: Effects of Performance Information Ambiguity," *Academy of Management Journal* 40, no. 3 (1997): 603–25.

6. "Does the Media Influence How We Perceive Women in Leadership?," Rockefeller Foundation, https://assets.rockefellerfoundation.org/app /uploads/20161028122206/100x25_MediaLanguage_report1.pdf.

7. Tom Huddleston Jr., "You'd Be Smart to Buy Stock in Companies with Women on Their Boards," *Fortune*, December 7, 2015, http://fortune .com/2015/12/07/female-board-directors-returns/.

8. "Large-Cap Companies with at Least One Woman on the Board Have Outperformed Their Peer Group with No Women on the-Board by 26% over the Last Six Years, According to a Report by Credit Suisse Research Institute," Credit Suisse, July 31, 2012, https://www.credit -suisse.com/corporate/en/articles/media-releases/42035-201207.html.

9. Marcus Noland, Tyler Moran, and Barbara Kotschwar, "New Peterson Institute Research on over 21,000 Companies Globally Finds Women in Corporate Leadership Can Significantly Increase Profitability," Peterson Institute for International Economics, February 8, 2016, https://www.piie.com/newsroom/press-releases/new-peterson -institute-research-over-21000-companies-globally-finds-women.

10. Cristian L. Dezsö and David Gaddis Ross, "Does Female Representation in Top Management Improve Firm Performance? A Panel Data Investigation," *Strategic Management Journal* 33, no. 9 (2012): 1072–89.

11. Vivian Hunt, Dennis Layton, and Sara Prince, "Why Diversity Matters," McKinsey & Company, January 2015, https://www.mckinsey.com /business-functions/organization/our-insights/why-diversity-matters.

12. "Why It Pays to Invest in Gender Diversity," Morgan Stanley, May 11, 2016, http://www.morganstanley.com/ideas/gender-diversity-investment -framework.

13. "Delivering Through Diversity," McKinsey & Company, January 2018, https://www.mckinsey.com/~/media/McKinsey/Business%20Functions /Organization/Our%20Insights/Delivering%20through%20diversity /Delivering-through-diversity_full-report.ashx.

14. Michael L. McDonald and James D. Westphal, "Access Denied: Low Mentoring of Women and Minority First-Time Directors and Its Negative Effects on Appointments to Additional Boards," *Academy of Management Journal* 56, no. 4 (2013): 1169–198.

15. Malcolm Gladwell, *Blink: The Power of Thinking Without Thinking* (New York: Little Brown and Company, 2006).

16. Eric Luis Uhlmann and Geoffrey L. Cohen, "Constructed Criteria: Redefining Merit to Justify Discrimination," *Psychological Science* 16, no. 6 (2005): 474–80.

Chapter 5: Leadership Strategies for Meritocracy Managers

1. Lauren Orsini, "Why GitHub's CEO Ditched Its Divisive 'Meritocracy' Rug," Business Insider, January 24, 2014, https://www.businessinsider .com/githubs-ceo-ditches-meritocracy-rug-2014-1.

2. Fast Company Staff, "Would the GitHub Debacle Happen at a Traditional Company?," Fast Company, May 1, 2014, https://www.fastcompany.com /3029962/would-the-github-debacle-happen-at-a-traditional-company.

3. Michael L. McDonald and James D. Westphal, "Access Denied: Low Mentoring of Women and Minority First-Time Directors and Its Negative Effects on Appointments to Additional Boards," *Academy of Management Journal* 56, no. 4 (2013): 1169–198.

4. Seung Ho Park and Michael E. Gordon, "Publication Records and Tenure Decisions in the Field of Strategic Management," *Strategic Management Journal* 17, no. 2 (1996): 109–28.

5. Caroline O'Donovan, "The Woman Hired to Fix GitHub's Troubled Culture Is Leaving, and Employees Are Worried," BuzzFeed News, July 14, 2017, https://www.buzzfeednews.com/article/carolineodonovan /an-executive-departure-at-github-reignites-employee.

6. Sylvia Ann Hewlett, Melinda Marshall, and Laura Sherbin, "How Diversity Can Drive Innovation," *Harvard Business Review*, December 2013, https://hbr.org/2013/12/how-diversity-can-drive-innovation.

7. Cedric Herring, "Does Diversity Pay?: Race, Gender, and the Business Case for Diversity," *American Sociological Review* 74, no. 2 (2009): 208–24.

8. Christine Wennerås and Agnes Wold, "Nepotism and Sexism in Peer-Review," *Nature* 7, no. 4 (May 1997): 46–52.

9. "Winning the Fight for Female Talent: How to Gain the Diversity Edge Through Inclusive Recruitment," PricewaterhouseCoopers, https://www.pwc.com/femaletalent.

10. Anne Fisher, "Note to Executives: Your Employees Are in the Dark," *Fortune*, April 30, 2013, http://fortune.com/2013/04/30/note-to -executives-your-employees-are-in-the-dark/.

11. "New Survey from Kimble: American Workers Care About the Well-Being of Their Employers Yet Lack Critical Insight into Business Performance," Kimble Applications, November 16, 2017, https:// www.kimbleapps.com/2017/11/new-survey-from-kimble-american -workers-care-about-the-well-being-of-their-employers-yet-lack -critical-insight-into-business-performance/.

12. "Redefining Business Success in a Changing World: CEO Survey," PricewaterhouseCoopers, January 2016, https://www.pwc.com/gx/en /ceo-survey/2016/landing-page/pwc-19th-annual-global-ceo-survey.pdf.

13. Claire Armstrong, Patrick C. Flood, James P. Guthrie, et al., "The Impact of Diversity and Equality Management on Firm Performance: Beyond High Performance Work Systems," *Human Resource Management* 49, no. 6 (2010): 977–98.

14. Adam D. Galinsky, Andrew R. Todd, Astrid C. Homan, et al., "Maximizing the Gains and Minimizing the Pains of Diversity: A Policy Perspective," *Perspectives on Psychological Science* 10, no. 6 (2015): 742–48.

15. Andrew K. Schnackenberg and Edward C. Tomlinson, "Organizational Transparency: A New Perspective on Managing Trust in Organization-

Stakeholder Relationships," *Journal of Management* 42, no. 7 (2016): 1784–810.

16. Marjorie Armstrong-Stassen and Francine Schlosser, "Perceived Organizational Membership and Retention of Older Workers," *Journal of Organizational Behavior* 32, no. 2 (2011): 319–44. Christina L. Stamper and Suzanne S. Masterson, "Insider or Outsider? How Employee Perceptions of Insider Status Affect Their Work Behavior," *Journal of Organizational Behavior* 23, no. 8 (2002): 875–94.

17. Erik Larson, "How to Use Inclusive Decision-Making to Drive Innovation and Performance," Cloverpop, June 19, 2018, https://www .cloverpop.com/blog/how-to-use-inclusive-decision-making-to-drive -innovation-and-performance.

18. Stephen M. R. Covey with Rebecca R. Merrill, *The Speed of Trust: The One Thing That Changes Everything* (New York: Simon & Schuster, 2006).

Chapter 6: Culture Crusader

1. Michael Klug and James P. Bagrow, "Understanding the Group Dynamics and Success of Teams," *Royal Society Open Science* 3, no. 4 (2016): 160007.

2. Katherine W. Phillips, Gregory B. Northcraft, and Margaret A. Neale, "Surface-Level Diversity and Decision-Making in Groups: When Does Deep-Level Similarity Help?," *Group Processes & Intergroup Relations* 9, no. 4 (2006): 467–82.

3. Jeffrey M. O'Brien, "The PayPal Mafia," *Fortune*, November 13, 2007, https://fortune.com/2007/11/13/paypal-mafia/. Tamsin McMahon, "What's Behind the Tech Industry's Toxic Masculinity Problem? Inside the Valley of the Bros," *The Globe and Mail*, July 21, 2017, https://www .theglobeandmail.com/technology/toxic-masculinity-in-silicon-valley /article35759481/.

4. Sarah E. Gaither, Evan P. Apfelbaum, Hannah J. Birnbaum, et al., "Mere Membership in Racially Diverse Groups Reduces Conformity," *Social Psychological and Personality Science* 9, no. 4 (2018): 402–10.

5. Michael Flood, "Australian Study Reveals the Dangers of 'Toxic Masculinity' to Men and Those Around Them," The Conversation, October 15, 2018, http://theconversation.com/australian-study-reveals-the-dangers-of-toxic-masculinity-to-men-and-those-around-them-104694.

6. Julie Creswell and Kevin Draper, "5 More Nike Executives Are Out Amid Inquiry into Harassment Allegations," *New York Times*, May 8, 2018, https://www.nytimes.com/2018/05/08/business/nike-harassment.html. Chavie Lieber, "Did Nike's 'Frat Boy Culture' Lead to the Departures of Two Executives?," Racked, March 16, 2018, https://www.racked.com/2018/3/16/17129110/nike-trevor-edwards-workplace-misconduct. "Nike Accused of 'Pattern' of Racial Discrimination in New Lawsuit," The Fashion Law, March 22, 2019, http://www.thefashionlaw.com/home/nike-accused-of-pattern-of-racial-discrimination-in-new-lawsuit.

7. Sridhar Natarajan and Gillian Tan, "A Credit Suisse Banker, an Intern and a Reckoning for Wall Street Culture," *The Australian Financial Review Magazine*, July 12, 2018, https://www.afr.com/work-and-careers/management/a-credit-suisse-banker-an-intern-and-a-reckoning-for-wall-street-culture-20180712-h12l2v.

8. Ben Child, "Disgraced Banker Jordan Belfort: Wolf of Wall Street Is a 'Cautionary Tale,'" *The Guardian*, January 22, 2014, https://www.theguardian.com/film/2014/jan/22/jordan-belfort-wolf-of-wall-street-depiction.

9. Vladas Griskevicius, Michelle N. Shiota, and Samantha L. Neufeld, "Influence of Different Positive Emotions on Persuasion Processing: A Functional Evolutionary Approach," *Emotion* 10, no. 2 (2010): 190–206.

10. Khadeeja Safdar, "Under Armour's #MeToo Moment: No More Strip Clubs on Company Dime," *Wall Street Journal*, November 5, 2018, https://www.wsj.com/articles/under-armours-metoo-moment-no-more-strip-clubs-on-company-dime-1541450209.

11. Emily Chang, *Brotopia: Breaking Up the Boys' Club of Silicon Valley* (New York: Portfolio/Penguin, 2019).

12. Sarah J. Gervais, Theresa K. Vescio, and Jill Allen, "When What You See Is What You Get: The Consequences of the Objectifying Gaze for Women and Men," *Psychology of Women Quarterly* 35, no. 1 (2011): 5–17. Sarah J. Gervais, Theresa K. Vescio, Jens Förster, et al., "Seeing Women as Objects: The Sexual Body Part Recognition Bias," *European Journal of Social Psychology* 42, no. 6 (2012): 743–53.

13. Bethany L. Peters and Edward Stringham, "No Booze? You May Lose: Why Drinkers Earn More Money than Nondrinkers," *Journal of Labor Research* 27, no. 3 (2006): 411–21.

14. Paul Bradley Carr, "'We Call That Boob-er:' The Four Most Awful Things Travis Kalanick Said in His *GQ* Profile," Pando, February 27, 2014, https://pando.com/2014/02/27/we-call-that-boob-er-the-four-most-awful-things-travis-kalanick-said-in-his-gq-profile/.

15. Johana Bhuiyan, "With Just Her Words, Susan Fowler Brought Uber to Its Knees," Vox, December 6, 2017, https://www.vox.com/2017/12/6/16680602/susan-fowler-uber-engineer-recode-100-diversity-sexual-harassment.

16. Hayley Tsukayama, "Uber Founder Travis Kalanick Sued, Accused of Fraud," *Washington Post*, August 10, 2017, https://www.washingtonpost.com/news/the-switch/wp/2017/08/10/uber-founder-travis-kalanick-sued-for-fraud/.

Chapter 7: Leadership Strategies for Culture Crusaders

1. Benjamin Edelman, Michael Luca, and Dan Svirsky, "Racial Discrimination in the Sharing Economy: Evidence from a Field Experiment," *American Economic Journal: Applied Economics* 9, no. 2 (2017): 1–22.

2. Jordan Lebeau, "Racial Discrimination Suit Against Airbnb Should Be Settled by Private Arbitration, Says Federal Judge," *Forbes*, November 2, 2016, https://www.forbes.com/sites/jordanlebeau/2016/11/02/racial-discrimination-suit-against-airbnb-should-be-settled-by-private-arbitration-says-federal-judge/#456f6a4214b7.

3. Olivia Solon, "Airbnb Host Who Canceled Reservation Using Racist

Comment Must Pay $5,000," *The Guardian*, July 13, 2017, https://
www.theguardian.com/technology/2017/jul/13/airbnb-california
-racist-comment-penalty-asian-american.

4. "How Airbnb Is Building Its Culture Through Belonging," Culture
   Amp, https://blog.cultureamp.com/how-airbnb-is-building-its-culture
   -through-belonging.

5. Cristian L. Dezsö and David Gaddis Ross, "Does Female Representation
   in Top Management Improve Firm Performance? A Panel Data
   Investigation," *Strategic Management Journal* 33, no. 9 (2012): 1072–89.

6. Orlando Richard, Amy McMillan, Ken Chadwick, and Sean Dwyer,
   "Employing an Innovation Strategy in Racially Diverse Workforces:
   Effects on Firm Performance," *Group & Organization Management* 28,
   no. 1 (2003): 107–6.

7. Richard C. Mayer, Richard S. Warr, and Jing Zhao, "Do Pro-Diversity
   Policies Improve Corporate Innovation?," *Financial Management* 47,
   no. 3 (2018): 617–50.

8. Katherine W. Phillips, Katie A. Liljenquist, and Margaret A. Neale,
   "Is the Pain Worth the Gain? The Advantages and Liabilities of
   Agreeing with Socially Distinct Newcomers," *Personality and Social
   Psychology Bulletin* 35, no. 3 (2009): 336–50.

9. Katherine W. Phillips, "How Diversity Makes Us Smarter," *Scientific
   American* 311, no. 4 (2014): 43–47.

10. Denise Lewin Loyd, Cynthia S. Wang, Katherine W. Phillips, and
    Robert B. Lount Jr., "Social Category Diversity Promotes Premeeting
    Elaboration: The Role of Relationship Focus," *Organization Science* 24,
    no. 3 (2013): 757–72.

11. Darrell G. Kirch, R. Kevin Grigsby, Wayne W. Zolko, et al., "Reinventing the
    Academic Health Center," *Academic Medicine* 80, no. 11 (2005): 980–89.

Chapter 8: Team Player

1. Shinsuke Eguchi, "Negotiating Hegemonic Masculinity: The
   Rhetorical Strategy of 'Straight-Acting' Among Gay Men," *Journal of
   Intercultural Communication Research* 38, no. 3 (2009): 193–209.

2. Belle Derks, Colette Van Laar, and Naomi Ellemers, "The Queen Bee Phenomenon: Why Women Leaders Distance Themselves from Junior Women," *The Leadership Quarterly* 27, no. 3 (2016): 456–69.

3. Rosabeth Moss Kanter, "Some Effects of Proportions on Group Life: Skewed Sex Ratios and Responses to Token Women," *American Journal of Sociology* 82, no. 5 (1977): 965–90.

4. Steve Harvey, *Act Like a Lady, Think Like a Man: What Men Really Think About Love, Relationships, Intimacy, and Commitment* (New York: Harper, 2009).

5. Sheryl Sandberg, *Lean In: Women, Work and the Will to Lead* (New York, Random House, 2015), 137–39.

6. Stefanie K. Johnson, Susan Elaine Murphy, Selamawit Zewdie, and Rebecca J. Reichard, "The Strong, Sensitive Type: Effects of Gender Stereotypes and Leadership Prototypes on the Evaluation of Male and Female Leaders," *Organizational Behavior and Human Decision Processes* 106, no. 1 (2008): 39–60.

7. Leah D. Sheppard and Karl Aquino, "Much Ado About Nothing? Observers' Problematization of Women's Same-Sex Conflict at Work," *Academy of Management Perspectives* 27, no. 1 (2013): 52–62.

8. Shona Ghosh, "Apple's First Diversity Boss Is Leaving—Not Long After Making Controversial Remarks About White Men," Business Insider, November 17, 2017, https://www.businessinsider.com/apple -diversity-vp-denise-young-smith-comments-white-men-2017-11.

9. Claude M. Steele, "Stereotyping and Its Threat Are Real," *American Psychologist* 53, no. 6 (1998): 680–81.

10. Crystal L. Hoyt, Stefanie K. Johnson, Susan Elaine Murphy, and Kerri Hogue Skinnell, "The Impact of Blatant Stereotype Activation and Group Sex-Composition on Female Leaders," *The Leadership Quarterly* 21, no. 5 (2010): 716–32.

11. Madeline E. Heilman, Michael C. Simon, and David P. Repper, "Intentionally Favored, Unintentionally Harmed? Impact of Sex-Based Preferential Selection on Self-Perceptions and Self-Evaluations," *Journal of Applied Psychology* 72, no. 1 (1987): 62–68.

12. Carol S. Dweck, *Mindset: The New Psychology of Success* (New York: Random House, 2006).

13. Judith M. Harackiewicz and Stacy J. Priniski, "Improving Student Outcomes in Higher Education: The Science of Targeted Intervention," *Annual Review of Psychology* 69 (2018): 409–35.

14. Alison M. Konrad, Vicki Kramer, and Sumru Erkut, "The Impact of Three or More Women on Corporate Boards," *Organizational Dynamics* 37, no. 2 (2008): 145–64.

15. Edward H. Chang, Katherine L. Milkman, Dolly Chugh, and Modupe Akinola, "Diversity Thresholds: How Social Norms, Visibility, and Scrutiny Relate to Group Composition," *Academy of Management Journal* 62, no. 1 (2019): 144–71.

16. Annamarie Houlis, "70% of Female Executives Feel Bullied by Women—Here's How to Stop It," Ladders, September 20, 2018, https://www.theladders.com/career-advice/70-of-women-feel-bullied -by-female-colleagues-heres-how-to-stop-it.

17. Staale Einarsen, Helge Hoel, and Guy Notelaers, "Measuring Exposure to Bullying and Harassment at Work: Validity, Factor Structure and Psychometric Properties of the Negative Acts Questionnaire-Revised," *Work & Stress*, 23, no. 1 (2009): 24–44.

18. Sridhar Natarajan and Gillian Tan, "A Credit Suisse Banker, an Intern and a Reckoning for Wall Street Culture," *The Australian Financial Review Magazine*, July 12, 2018, https://www.afr.com/work-and-careers/management/a -credit-suisse-banker-an-intern-and-a-reckoning-for-wall-street-culture -20180712-h12l2v.

19. Adam Grant, *Give and Take: A Revolutionary Approach to Success* (New York: Viking, 2013).

Chapter 9: Leadership Strategies for Team Players

1. "Marissa Mayer," Makers, https://www.youtube.com/watch?v =yTv2W7nP07U.

2. Nicole Lyn Pesce, "Marissa Mayer Bans Telecommuting at Yahoo! and Becomes the Mother of Dissension," *New York Daily News*, March 4,

2013, https://www.nydailynews.com/life-style/n-y-moms-react-yahoo
-ban-telecommuting-article-1.1277492.

3. Lara O'Reilly, "Female Tech CEO: Marissa Mayer's View on Gender
'Sets Us Back,'" Business Insider, March 9, 2015, https://www
.businessinsider.com/sama-group-ceo-leila-janah-criticizes-marissa
-mayers-view-on-gender-in-the-workplace-2015-3.

4. Matt Weinberger, "The Rise and Fall of Marissa Mayer, from the
Once-Beloved CEO of Yahoo to a $4.48 Billion Sale to Verizon,"
Business Insider, June 13, 2017, https://www.businessinsider.com
/yahoo-marissa-mayer-rise-and-fall-2017-6.

5. "980 Middlefield Road: Prescreening for PC Amendment," City
Council Staff Report, City of Palo Alto, https://www.cityofpaloalto
.org/civicax/filebank/documents/66766.

6. Samantha Murphy Kelly, "Marissa Mayer–Backed Startup Wants
$5,000 a Year for a VIP Family Playspace," CNN Business, May 9,
2019, https://www.cnn.com/2019/05/09/tech/the-wonder/index
.html.

7. Charles Duhigg, "What Google Learned from Its Quest to Build the
Perfect Team," The New York Times Magazine, February 25, 2016,
https://www.nytimes.com/2016/02/28/magazine/what-google-learned
-from-its-quest-to-build-the-perfect-team.html.

8. Amy Edmondson, "Psychological Safety and Learning Behavior in Work
Teams," Administrative Science Quarterly 44, no. 2 (1999): 350–83.

9. Ingrid M. Nembhard and Amy C. Edmondson, "Making It Safe:
The Effects of Leader Inclusiveness and Professional Status on
Psychological Safety and Improvement Efforts in Health Care
Teams," Journal of Organizational Behavior 27, no. 7 (2006): 941–66.

10. John M. Darley and Bibb Latané, "Bystander Intervention in
Emergencies: Diffusion of Responsibility," Journal of Personality and
Social Psychology 8, no. 4 (1968): 377–83.

11. Bibb Latané and John M. Darley, "Group Inhibition of Bystander
Intervention in Emergencies," Journal of Personality and Social
Psychology 10, no. 3 (1968): 215.

12. Brigid Schulte, "To Combat Harassment, More Companies Should Try Bystander Training," *Harvard Business Review*, October 31, 2018, https://hbr.org/2018/10/to-combat-harassment-more-companies -should-try-bystander-training.

13. "More Than 2/3 of Women Feel Bullied by Female Colleagues— Here's How to Stop It," GirlTalkHQ, October 16, 2018, https:// girltalkhq.com/more-than-2-3-of-women-feel-bullied-by-female -colleagues-heres-how-to-stop-it/.

Chapter 10: White Knight

1. Alexander M. Czopp, Aaron C. Kay, and Sapna Cheryan, "Positive Stereotypes Are Pervasive and Powerful," *Perspectives on Psychological Science* 10, no. 4 (2015): 451–63.

2. Ibid.

3. Stefanie K. Johnson, Susan Elaine Murphy, Selamawit Zewdie, and Rebecca J. Reichard, "The Strong, Sensitive Type: Effects of Gender Stereotypes and Leadership Prototypes on the Evaluation of Male and Female Leaders," *Organizational Behavior and Human Decision Processes* 106, no. 1 (2008): 39–60.

4. Juan M. Madera, Michelle R. Hebl, and Randi C. Martin, "Gender and Letters of Recommendation for Academia: Agentic and Communal Differences," *Journal of Applied Psychology* 94, no. 6 (2009): 1591–99.

5. Joseph Zajda, "Research on Discrimination and Self-Fulfilling Prophecy in Schools Globally," *Education and Society* 37, no. 1 (2019): 59–77.

6. Debra L. Oswald, Maha Baalbaki, and Mackenzie Kirkman, "Experiences with Benevolent Sexism: Scale Development and Associations with Women's Well-Being," *Sex Roles* 80, nos. 5–6 (2019): 362–80.

7. Aarti Ramaswami, George F. Dreher, Robert Bretz, and Carolyn Wiethoff, "Gender, Mentoring, and Career Success: The Importance of Organizational Context," *Personnel Psychology* 63, no. 2 (2010): 385–405.

8. Liz Wiseman, *Rookie Smarts: Why Learning Beats Knowing in the New Game of Work* (New York: Harper Business, 2014).

9. "Tool: Optimizing Mentoring Programs for Women of Color," Catalyst, December 5, 2012, https://www.catalyst.org/research/optimizing -mentoring-programs-for-women-of-color/.

10. "The Sponsor Dividend," Center for Talent Innovation, 2019, https:// www.talentinnovation.org/_private/assets/TheSponsorDividend_Key FindingsCombined-CTI.pdf.

Chapter 11: Leadership Strategies for White Knights

1. Christine E. Carmichael and Maureen H. McDonough, "Community Stories: Explaining Resistance to Street Tree-Planting Programs in Detroit, Michigan, USA," *Society & Natural Resources* 32, no. 5 (2019): 588–605.

2. Clayton M. Christensen, Efosa Ojomo, and Karen Dillon, *The Prosperity Paradox: How Innovation Can Lift Nations Out of Poverty* (New York: Harper Business, 2019).

3. Carmichael and McDonough, "Community Stories."

4. Matt Krentz, Olivier Wierzba, Katie Abouzahr, et al., "Five Ways Men Can Improve Gender Diversity at Work," Boston Consulting Group, October 10, 2017, https://www.bcg.com/en-us/publications/2017 /people-organization-behavior-culture-five-ways-men-improve-gender -diversity-work.aspx.

5. Richard P. Eibach and Thomas Keegan, "Free at Last? Social Dominance, Loss Aversion, and White and Black Americans' Differing Assessments of Racial Progress," *Journal of Personality and Social Psychology* 90, no. 3 (2006): 453–67. Richard P. Eibach and Joyce Ehrlinger, "'Keep Your Eyes on the Prize': Reference Points and Racial Differences in Assessing Progress Toward Equality," *Personality and Social Psychology Bulletin* 32, no. 1 (2006): 66–77. Michael L. McDonald and James D. Westphal, "Access Denied: Low Mentoring of Women and Minority First-Time Directors and Its Negative Effects on Appointments to Additional Boards," *Academy of Management Journal* 56, no. 4 (2013): 1169–198.

6. "On Pay Gap, Millennial Women Near Parity—for Now," Pew Research Center, December 11, 2013, https://www.pewsocialtrends .org/2013/12/11/on-pay-gap-millennial-women-near-parity-for-now/.

7. Daniel Goleman, *Emotional Intelligence* (New York: Bantam Books, 1995).

8. Phil Plait, "#YesAllWomen," Slate, May 27, 2014, https://slate.com
/technology/2014/05/not-all-men-how-discussing-womens-issues
-gets-derailed.html.

9. Albert Bandura, "Social-Learning Theory of Identificatory Processes,"
in *Handbook of Socialization Theory and Research*, ed. D. A. Goslin
(Chicago: Rand McNally, 1969), 213–62.

10. Robert Rosenthal and Lenore Jacobson, "Pygmalion in the
Classroom," *The Urban Review* 3, no. 1 (1968): 16–20.

11. Dov Eden and Abraham B. Shani, "Pygmalion Goes to Boot Camp:
Expectancy, Leadership, and Trainee Performance," *Journal of Applied
Psychology* 67, no. 2 (1982): 194–99.

12. Paul Whiteley, Thomas Sy, and Stefanie K. Johnson, "Leaders'
Conceptions of Followers: Implications for Naturally Occurring
Pygmalion Effects," *The Leadership Quarterly* 23, no. 5 (2012): 822–34.

13. Linda Babcock, Maria P. Recalde, Lise Vesterlund, and Laurie
Weingart, "Gender Differences in Accepting and Receiving Requests
for Tasks with Low Promotability," *American Economic Review* 107,
no. 3 (2017): 714–47.

14. Joan C. Williams and Marina Multhaup, "For Women and Minorities
to Get Ahead, Managers Must Assign Work Fairly," *Harvard Business
Review*, March 5, 2018, https://hbr.org/2018/03/for-women-and
-minorities-to-get-ahead-managers-must-assign-work-fairly.

15. Ibid.

16. Madeline E. Heilman and Julie J. Chen, "Same Behavior, Different
Consequences: Reactions to Men's and Women's Altruistic Citizenship
Behavior," *Journal of Applied Psychology* 90, no. 3 (2005): 431–41.

Chapter 12: Shepherd

1. Maw-Der Foo, David R. Hekman, Stefanie K. Johnson, and Wei Yang,
"Does Diversity-Valuing Behavior Result in Diminished Performance
Ratings for Non-White and Female Leaders?," *Academy of Management
Journal* 60, no. 2 (2017): 771–97.

2. *James Damore, David Gudeman, Manual Amador, Stephen McPherson, and Michael Burns, individually and on behalf of all others similarly situated, Plaintiffs, v. Google, LLC, a Delaware limited liability company; and DOES 1-10, Defendants*, Superior Court of California, April 18, 2018, https://www.dhillonlaw.com/wp-content/uploads /2018/04/20180418-Damore-et-al.-v.-Google-FAC_Endorsed.pdf, 52.

3. Stefanie K. Johnson, "What the Science Actually Says About Gender Gaps in the Workplace," *Harvard Business Review*, August 17, 2017, https://hbr.org/2017/08/what-the-science-actually-says-about-gender -gaps-in-the-workplace.

4. Grace Donnelly, "Survey Confirms What Diversity Professionals Have Long Suspected: People Think Inclusion in the Workplace Hurts White Men," *Fortune*, September 28, 2017, https://fortune.com/2017/09/28 /survey-diversity-hurts-white-men/.

5. Stacy Jones, "White Men Account for 72% of Corporate Leadership at 16 of the Fortune 500 Companies," *Fortune*, June 9, 2017, http:// fortune.com/2017/06/09/white-men-senior-executives-fortune-500 -companies-diversity-data/.

6. Jonathan Howard, "Confirmation Bias, Motivated Cognition, the Backfire Effect," in *Cognitive Errors and Diagnostic Mistakes* (Cham, Switzerland: Springer, 2019), 57–58.

7. Ian M. Handley, Elizabeth R. Brown, Corinne A. Moss-Racusin, and Jessi L. Smith, "Quality of Evidence Revealing Subtle Gender Biases in Science Is in the Eye of the Beholder," *Proceedings of the National Academy of Sciences of the United States of America* 112, no. 43 (2015): 13201–06.

8. Peter G. Roma, Alan Silberberg, Angela M. Ruggiero, and Stephen J. Suomi, "Capuchin Monkeys, Inequity Aversion, and the Frustration Effect," *Journal of Comparative Psychology* 120, no. 1 (2006): 67–73.

9. Sally Ann Hewlett, Ripa Rashid, and Laura Sherbin, "When Employees Think the Boss Is Unfair, They're More Likely to Disengage and Leave," *Harvard Business Review*, August 1, 2017,

https://hbr.org/2017/08/when-employees-think-the-boss-is-unfair
-theyre-more-likely-to-disengage-and-leave.

10. Brenda Major, Alison Blodorn, and Gregory Major Blascovich,
    "The Threat of Increasing Diversity: Why Many White Americans
    Support Trump in the 2016 Presidential Election," *Group Processes &
    Intergroup Relations* 21, no. 6 (2018): 931–40.

11. Michael L. McDonald, Gareth D. Keeves, and James D. Westphal,
    "One Step Forward, One Step Back: White Male Top Manager
    Organizational Identification and Helping Behavior Toward Other
    Executives Following the Appointment of a Female or Racial Minority
    CEO," *Academy of Management Journal* 61, no. 2 (2018): 405–39.

Chapter 13: Leadership Strategies for Shepherds

1. Jo Wallace, "What Marketing Agencies Can Do Right Now to Make
   Diversity More than Just Talk," *The Drum*, December 7, 2017,
   https://www.thedrum.com/opinion/2017/12/07/what-marketing
   -agencies-can-do-right-now-make-diversity-more-just-talk.

2. Jim Edwards, "5 Male Ad Execs Are Considering a Discrimination
   Claim After Their Gay Female Boss Said She Would 'Obliterate' Her
   Company's Reputation as a Haven for Straight, White Men," Business
   Insider, November 17, 2018, https://www.businessinsider.com/jwt-jo
   -wallace-straight-white-men-consider-a-discrimination-claim-2018-11.

3. "When Women Thrive: An Evidence Based Approach to Diversity and
   Inclusion," Mercer, https://www.mercer.com/our-thinking/when
   -women-thrive.html.

4. Chuck Shelton and David A. Thomas, "The Study on White Men
   Leading Through Diversity & Inclusion: Results Report," Greatheart
   Leader Labs, February 2013, http://www.whitemensleadershipstudy
   .com/pdf/WMLS%20Results%20Report.pdf.

5. Ann Friedman, "Shine Theory: Why Powerful Women Make the
   Greatest Friends," *The Cut*, May 31, 2013, https://www.thecut.com
   /2013/05/shine-theory-how-to-stop-female-competition.html.

6. Chimamanda Ngozi Adichie, "The Danger of a Single Story," TED

Talk, July 2009, https://www.ted.com/talks/chimamanda_ngozi
_adichie_the_danger_of_a_single_story/transcript?language=en.

7. George Yancy, *Look, a White!: Philosophical Essays on Whitenesss* (Philadelphia: Temple University Press, 2012).

8. Blythe Roberson, *How to Date Men When You Hate Men* (New York: Flatiron Books, 2019).

9. Dee Dee Myers, *Why Women Should Rule the World* (New York: Harper, 2008).

Chapter 14: Optimist

1. Dan Ariely, *Predictably Irrational: The Hidden Forces That Shape Our Decisions* (New York: Harper, 2008).

2. Terri Imbarlina Patak, "Ask the Legal: Do Employers Have to Pay Employees for Smoke Breaks?," Dickie, McCamey & Chilcote, P.C., https://www.dmclaw.com/events-media/do-employers-have-to-pay -employees-for-smoke-breaks/.

3. HaloCigs, "You Won't Believe The Staggering Amount of Time Wasted on Workplace Smoke Breaks," Ladders, March 1, 2018, https://www.theladders.com/career-advice/you-wont-believe-the -staggering-amount-of-time-wasted-on-workplace-smoke-breaks.

4. Amanda Glenn, "What You Need to Know About Pumping at Work Laws," Exclusive Pumping, May 15, 2019, https://exclusivepumping .com/pumping-at-work-laws/.

5. Heather Stockton and Juliet Bourke, "From Diversity to Inclusion: Shift from Compliance to Diversity as a Business Strategy," Deloitte, 2019, https://www2.deloitte.com/global/en/pages/human-capital /articles/diversity-to-inclusion.html.

6. Lisa H. Nishii, "The Benefits of Climate for Inclusion for Gender-Diverse Groups," *Academy of Management Journal* 56, no. 6 (2013): 1754–74.

7. Josh Bersin, "Why Companies Fail to Engage Today's Workforce: The Overwhelmed Employee," *Forbes*, March 15, 2014, https://www.forbes .com/sites/joshbersin/2014/03/15/why-companies-fail-to-engage -todays-workforce-the-overwhelmed-employee/#65281ca44726.

8. Christie Smith and Stephanie Turner, "The Radical Transformation of Diversity and Inclusion: The Millennial Influence," Deloitte, 2015, https://www2.deloitte.com/content/dam/Deloitte/us/Documents /about-deloitte/us-inclus-millennial-influence-120215.pdf.

9. Bersin, "Why Companies Fail to Engage Today's Workforce."

10. "Diversity, Equity and Inclusion," William and Flora Hewlett Foundation, https://hewlett.org/diversity-equity-inclusion/.

11. Juliet Bourke and Andrea Espedido, "Why Inclusive Leaders Are Good for Organizations and How to Become One," *Harvard Business Review*, March 29, 2019, https://hbr.org/2019/03/why -inclusive-leaders-are-good-for-organizations-and-how-to-become -one.

12. Bersin, "Why Companies Fail to Engage Today's Workforce."

Chapter 15: Leadership Strategies for Optimists

1. "#BrandsGetReal: Championing Change in the Age of Social Media," Sprout Social, January 9, 2018, https://sproutsocial.com/insights /data/championing-change-in-the-age-of-social-media/.

2. Edwin A. Locke and Gary P. Latham, "New Directions in Goal-Setting Theory," *Current Directions in Psychological Science* 15, no. 5 (2006): 265–68.

3. Emilio J. Castilla, "Accounting for the Gap: A Firm Study Manipulating Organizational Accountability and Transparency in Pay Decisions," *Organization Science* 26, no. 2 (2015): 311–33.

4. Stefanie K. Johnson, David R. Hekman, and Elsa T. Chan, "If There's Only One Woman in Your Candidate Pool, There's Statistically No Chance She'll Be Hired," *Harvard Business Review*, April 26, 2016, https://hbr.org/2016/04/if-theres-only-one-woman-in-your -candidate-pool-theres-statistically-no-chance-shell-be-hired.

5. Jennifer Mogeland, "PepsiCo's Billion-Dollar Commitment," Hispanic Executive, September 26, 2012, https://hispanicexecutive .com/pepsicos-billion-dollar-commitment/.

6. Christie Smith and Stephanie Turner, "The Radical Transformation of Diversity and Inclusion: The Millennial Influence," Deloitte, https://

www2.deloitte.com/content/dam/Deloitte/us/Documents/about
-deloitte/us-inclus-millennial-influence-120215.pdf.

7. Holly Schroth, "Are You Ready for Gen Z in the Workplace?,"
California Management Review 61, no. 3 (2019): 5–18.

8. Darnell Hunt, Ana-Christina Ramón, Michael Tran, et al.,
"Hollywood Diversity Report 2018: Five Years of Progress and
Missed Opportunities," UCLA College of Social Sciences, https://
socialsciences.ucla.edu/wp-content/uploads/2018/02/UCLA
-Hollywood-Diversity-Report-2018-2-27-18.pdf.

9. Patrick Hipes, "'Grey's Anatomy' Scrubbing In for Record-Breaking
Episode This Week," Deadline, February 26, 2019, https://deadline
.com/2019/02/greys-anatomy-episode-history-medical-drama-record
-abc-1202565863/#!.

10. Hunt et al., "Hollywood Diversity Report 2018."

11. Venkat Kuppuswamy and Peter Younkin, "Testing the Theory of
Consumer Discrimination as an Explanation for the Lack of Minority
Hiring in Hollywood Films," *Management Science* (in press).

Chapter 16: My Inclusify Journey

1. David A. M. Peterson, Lori A. Biederman, David Andersen, et al.,
"Mitigating Gender Bias in Student Evaluations of Teaching," *PLoS
ONE* 14, no. 5 (2019): e0216241.

INDEX

Note: Italic page numbers refer to charts and illustrations.

ABOUT THE AUTHOR

DR. STEFANIE K. JOHNSON is an author, a professor, and a keynote speaker who studies the intersection of leadership and diversity, focusing on how unconscious bias affects the evaluation of leaders and strategies leaders can use to mitigate bias. She is member of the MG 100 Coaches and works with the best companies in the world to create more-inclusive leaders. Dr. Johnson has extensive consulting experience and has created and delivered leadership development training with an emphasis on evidence-based practice.

As an associate professor at the University of Colorado Boulder's Leeds School of Business, Dr. Johnson teaches undergraduate and graduate students focused on leadership and inclusion. She is also passionate about disseminating her work more broadly and has taught two LinkedIn Learning courses on how to increase diversity and inclusion in corporations. She has received $3,800,000 in external grant funding to study leadership and create leadership development programs. Her safety leadership course was adopted by the OSHA 30 and was taken by 70,000 students in its first two years. She is an active researcher and has published sixty journal articles and book chapters in outlets *Journal of Applied Psychology* and *The Academy of Management Journal*.

Dr. Johnson is also a frequent contributor to the *Harvard Business Review* and an in-demand keynote speaker. She has presented her work at more than 170 meetings around the world, including at the White House for a 2016 summit on diversity in corporate America on National Equal Pay Day. Media outlets featuring Dr. Johnson's work include the *Economist, Newsweek, Time,* the *Wall Street Journal,*

Bloomberg, *HuffPost*, *Washington Post*, *Quartz*, *Discover*, CNN, ABC, NBC, CNBC. She has appeared on Fox, ABC, NBC, CNN, and CNN International.

Dr. Johnson lives in the Boulder Bubble in Colorado with her biology professor husband, two young kiddos, and two old kitties.